FOREWORD

My first attempt at writing was **THE FLYING DUTCHMAN**, a large yearly diary that contained over 2000 photos, Dutch history, genealogy and family information from my birth up to the year 2018. Following that I wrote a short autobiography titled **JAAK**. It basically outlined memories of my being a young Dutch boy during the German occupation of Holland during WWII and ended with my family moving to America in 1948. With this effort I will add more memories from that time period and elaborate on some childhood experiences. Included will be historical references, Dutch customs and a variety of culinary delights we enjoyed. I hope the reader will find these added memories interesting.

CONTENTS

Chapter I	Before my memories	1
Chapter II	The start of WWII	7
Chapter III	The move from our first home	24
Chapter IV	The flooding of the Polders and our village	34
Chapter V	The end of the War	56
Chapter VI	Rebuilding and visits	63
Chapter VII	Dutch customs and foods	75
Chapter VIII	School and sports	85
Chapter IX	Cousin Neeltje	93
Chapter X	Girls, boats and growing up	103
Chapter XI	Our departure and arrival in America	117

Chapter I -- BEFORE MY MEMORIES

Before there were memories there was a beginning. That beginning was my mother and father being married in 1934 when both were in their twenties. Dad was born in 1907 and mom in 1911. The courting process that brought them together began when dad used to help his buddy pick up milk at big dairy farms. My mother worked at one of those farms and for some reason would always be around when dad was on the truck picking up milk cans. Their relationship began as it was discovered they both loved to dance and dad asking mom out. Mom and dad had planned to marry in 1933 but there was no place for them to live.

My parents wedding

Following an extensive search a small house on the Ruigendyk road, leading to the town of Oudenhoorn, became available to rent. Not long after moving in my brother Cor and I were born in that house.

The house where I was born

Ruigendyk is about four miles from the village of Oudenhoorn. Oudenhoorn is located in the middle of a dyked island, Voorne en Putten, which is near the huge Seaport of Rotterdam.

Island of Voorne en Putten --- Location of Oudenhoorn

As told by my mother, she was nine months pregnant and on a sunny day in October while in the garden gathering vegetables for the evening dinner her water broke. Since I was her first child that was totally unexpected and she called out to the neighbor lady who then helped mom into the house. A midwife was summoned and a couple of hours later I was born. The date was October 2, 1936, three years before World War II was started by Germany invading Poland in 1939.

I was named Jaak after my dad's sister Dirkje's son. Mom told me my love for gardening must be due to almost being born in the garden. We have always had a garden at homes where we lived and I still do gardening today --- at 86 years old.

My younger brother Cor was born March 26, 1938. Though there was only 18 months difference in our ages Cor and I grew up close to the same height. Early photographs show how close my brother Cor and I were in size. We had completely different temperaments, however, and our many differences led to a lot of fighting during our early years.

Jaak and Cor

It seems Cor inherited genes from our grandpa Snoek, my mother's dad. They had about the same temperament and even looked somewhat alike. Both Cor and grandpa Snoek were wiry and feisty.

Cor, from an early age was always involved in anything sports related and remained physically active throughout his adult life, either playing or coaching.

For me, sports were not utmost on my list of goals. I was always more in tune to academics, mechanics and building things. Later in life those same interests motivated my many business and personal ventures. I don't really know from whom I received my genes except possibly my mother. She was the family business head and bookkeeper and I suspect some of those same traits must have passed on to me.

Dad started working when he was thirteen years old and just barely out of school. Mom, a year younger than dad, worked for a local farmer as a helper to the farmer's wife. Dad worked for his sister Dina's husband, Izak Van Hennik, who was a potato buyer and employed a number of people. Izak would buy potatoes from area farmers, load them up in the fields, haul them to his large storage facilities for sorting and eventually put in gunnysacks to be sold to large distributors in the city. It was a year round operation. Dina and Izak lived in a large house in the village of Oudenhoorn.

After working at Izak's for some time dad became qualified to drive one of the company trucks. He started with local pick-ups but eventually went into regular driving because Izak's son who also wanted to drive didn't like to make long hauls that caused him to get home late at night or the labor involved in unloading the trucks. Driving a truck was only part of a driver's job as sacks of potatoes weighing about a hundred pounds each had to be unloaded at destination. I really don't know how my dad did it because he was not a large man --- but he did.

Dad's truck

Izak's business was less than a mile from where mom and dad lived so it was very convenient. Dad could either walk or ride his bicycle to work. The Van Henniks also owned a cafe across the road from their business. It was a sort of restaurant/beer hall establishment where many of the locals gathered after work and on weekends. Next to their business was a small train station for the local steam train that ran several times a day to Rotterdam, which is twenty-five miles away. It was a major mode of transportation since working people would either bicycle to work or take the train. Not many people had automobiles as only the wealthy could afford them.

Holland is a land of many bicycles. Today seventeen million people live in Holland and there are over twenty two million bicycles. The use of bicycles for transportation started in the late 1800s and at the turn of the century bicycles paths soon followed. Bicycles have right of way over automobile traffic and popular due to their extremely low accident rates and affordable to the average person.

Typical bicycle path   Families on bicycles

Bicycle parking at train station

Except for the references to bicycling in Holland, this chapter is largely based upon the few photographs taken during that time and the many loving stories passed on to me by family and friends. Were it not for their cherished input, much of this chapter would not have been possible

I have no solid recollection of the first four years of my life and the memories shared in this book date from the mid 1940s forward.

Chapter II -- THE START OF WORLD WAR II

The Dutch wished to remain neutral with Germany but were met with Germany's announcement of its intent to invade lowland areas of Holland and Belgium. In response to this threat Holland rushed its army, many on bicycles, and what limited armored vehicles it had to defend its border. But, sadly, the Dutch were ill prepared for war as its soldiers and mechanized army was no match to the massive German army --- an army equipped with modern tanks, vehicles and weapons.

Dutch Army rushing to defend its border

Dutch armored vehicle at onset of WW II'

On May 10, 1940, Germany officially started war with Holland but did not invade as expected. While Dutch troops amassed at their border Germany dropped thousands of paratroopers behind the Dutch lines. Because Holland had a great road system for automobiles and bicycle paths throughout the country, German paratroopers landed with bicycles for ready mobilization.

German paratroopers with folding bicycles

NAZIS INVADE HOLLAND, BELGIUM, LUXEMBOURG BY LAND AND AIR; DIKES OPENED; ALLIES RUSH AID

New York Times headlines

Upon landing, the German soldiers deployed rapidly and took over most local government positions in a matter of a few days. But the Dutch were not ready to surrender. Germany then bombed the huge industrial complex and seaport of Rotterdam. The bombing flattened a large part of the city and Germany threatened to bomb Amsterdam next. The Queen and Parliament surrendered in just five days. I can still remember the bombing of Rotterdam. We could see German planes in the distance and hear what sounded like thunder.

Rotterdam after the bombing by the Germans that brought Holland to a surrender in just five days

Holland had a very small Air Force, about 150 airplanes, at the start of its five-day war with Germany. During that short war, most became casualties as result of German air superiority. All 16 of Dutch bombers were shot down, as were 30 of its 36 Fokker XXI single seat fighters. Also shot down were 17 of its 35 twin engine Fokker GI fighters, with most of the rest destroyed on the ground. A couple managed to be flown to England to join in its fight with Germany.

Valiant Dutch pilots and highly effective anti-aircraft fire from the Dutch Army took a toll on the invading German Luftwaffe, however. Germany lost 350 aircraft in its conquest of Holland but the cost of defense was equally steep as Dutch pilots suffered a 95% casualty rate. The air war above Europe proved even more horrific with the loss of over 250,000 Allied and German airmen.

Fokker G1 – Most prominent Dutch aircraft prior to WWII

Dutch Fokker XXI fending off German Messerschmidt BF 109

With only light fighting on the border between the Dutch and Germans it didn't take long for the Germans to drive their mechanized army, primarily tanks and trucks, into Holland.

The Dutch Royal Family and many government officials escaped the German invasion by flying to England and from there on to Canada where they stayed during the war.

German tanks and trucks as they cross the border

The beginning of war years in Europe was about the time of my earliest recollections. My brother Cor was two years younger than I was and the war didn't mean anything to him, but my memories are quite vivid.

Dad had told us the Germans would be coming to the island soon, even to our small town out in the countryside. He was just not sure when. Then, one day in May of 1940, I heard a rumble in the distance and the noise was heading toward our house. I was supposed to be watching my little brother Cor who was playing with his little wheelbarrow in front of the house next to the road. The rumbling noise got louder and louder and I soon saw a large column of trucks coming down our road. As the column drew near I could see it was being led by some officers in a jeep sort of vehicle. I was fascinated by all the heavy military equipment, especially the trucks carrying soldiers, and in a trance, I froze as I watched. All of a sudden the entire column stopped right in front of our house. In the excitement I had not been paying attention to Cor and he had wandered out onto the road with his little wheelbarrow. He was right smack in the middle of the road when the column stopped. I then saw one of the German officers get out of the jeep and walk over to pick up Cor and his wheel borrow. By that time mom had come out of the house wondering what was going on outside. The grinning officer walked over, handed Cor to mom, then jumped back in his jeep and the column moved on. Cor was three at the time and I was five. That was my first encounter with the Germans and most memorable. I still recall much of the events of that day over 80 years ago, as well as the scolding I got from my mom for not watching Cor.

German truck convoy

I was five years old when I started school in 1941. Our house was about four miles from the village of Oudenhoorn. Dad taught me to ride my own little bicycle so I could ride it to school with some of the neighborhood kids.

Strange how the word 'kindergarten' is common to both the Dutch and English languages. 'Kinder' in Dutch means a 'child' and 'garten' in English is 'garden' --- though a garden in Dutch is called a 'tuin', a place where you grow things.

The area where we lived was primarily agricultural and it was an important part of our education to learn the basics of growing crops. Each child in kindergarten had a little garden plot behind the school where they grew vegetables. We went to school five full eight-hour days and a half-day on Saturday. This method allowed the Dutch to acquire the equivalent of an eighth grade education by grade six.

The island on which we lived is a series of enclosed dykes where water had been pumped out by windmills or conventional pumps. This method of reclaiming land had started back in Roman times. The entire area is part of a huge delta where the Maas, Waal and Rhine rivers converge into the North Sea. The soil is very rich with nutrients that flow in from as far as Switzerland then settle in the delta. Water is very shallow most of the time, except for high tides when everything is covered. Being such, it didn't take huge dykes to enclose the seawater. After pumping out sea water a few years of rain dilutes salt water in the soil and it is ready for growing crops. These enclosed areas were called 'polders' in Dutch.

1:The village circle and church   2:My school   3:Canal where the 'bathtub boat' was launched   4:Our family home prior to leaving for America

The surrounding dykes are considered intermediate dykes and usually have roads on top. On the North Sea side there are large dykes that protect the polders from high tides and storms. Because of the pounding sea these dykes are very high and covered with huge rocks. Storms are very frequent on the North Sea and there are always some broken dykes after bad storms.

Our little village of Oudenhoorn started in the 1300's. When a church was built there in 1363 Oudenhoorn officially became a town. Oudenhoorn is a well-laid out village. A church is located in the center of the village, which is surrounded by a moat that has several bridges crossing over it to an encircling road. Stores and other businesses were soon built to accommodate village needs. Some of these are; a bakery, sundries store, flower shop, cafe and, of course, a beer hall.

The town is the center of social life for the surrounding area and even has a bandstand that extends over the church moat where music is played summer months. Oudenhoorn has grown, but very slowly, and having visited several times since leaving Holland in 1948 the core village still looks about the same. Modern structures have since been built on roads leading to the town circle.

Church and road into Oudenhoorn

My dad was the fourth child in a family of sixteen children, ten sisters and six brothers. Two of the children were from a previous marriage as grandpa Vander Waal lost his first wife at an early age. My dad's parents lived near the village of Oudenhoorn, about three miles away and not far from the big sea dyke. They had a small farm with cows, pigs and lots of chickens. The farm was always a gathering place for family. In his later years grandpa Vander Waal would hire out his wagon pulled by a horse to haul things for people.

Mom's parents, the Snoeks, had nine children, seven boys and two girls. Mom was the older of the two girls by 12 years. They lived near the village of Niewenhoorn, which is about ten miles from Oudenhoorn. Their house was right on the Voornse Canal, a man made waterway about 300 feet wide and built in the 1830's as a shortcut for ships taking produce from the islands to Rotterdam. The canal had a series of locks at each end to control the seawater.

On the southern end of the canal was Hellevoetsluis, a naval seaport that dates back to the 1700's. It was at one time the center of the Dutch Naval Fleet. Near the other end of the canal was the historic walled city of Den Briel, a fortress of a city that dates back to the 15th century. Fortresses at Hellevoetsluis and Den Briel experienced a lot of action during the "Eighty Year War" between Spain and Holland. .

Early Hellevoetsluis

The following page has an early map of Hellevoetsluis and photo of Hellevoetsluis today. Note the ramparts outline as they have not changed since the city's inception.

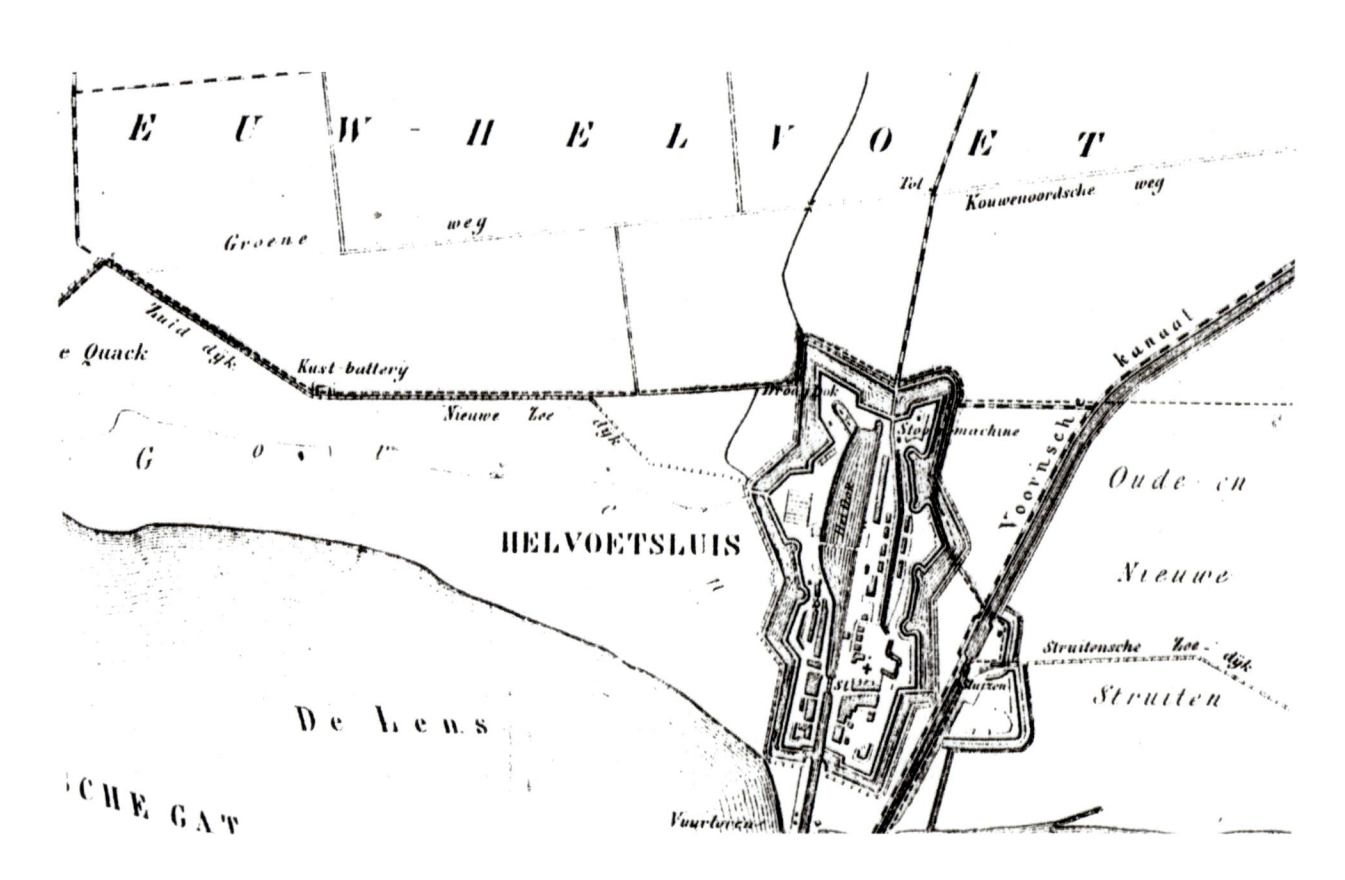

Helevoetsluis then

Helevoetsluis now

We kids loved to visit grandma Snoek because she was so much fun to be around. She would crack jokes, was very boisterous and always made us laugh. Grandpa Snoek was a foreman at a large diary farm nearby. He had a huge garden where he grew all sorts of crops and lots of flowers. Grandma loved to bake cakes and cookies and always had plenty in store. We would always leave there with a load of vegetables and grandma's goodies.

Grandma Snoek was the center of gossip in the area. All the delivery people; such as the mail man, milk man and sundry drivers, would stop by grandma's for a cup of tea or coffee, some goodies and to catch up on all the latest news and gossip.

Grandma and grandpa Snoek lived a typical Dutch style farmhouse with the barn and house combined as one. Whenever we stayed overnight there we would sleep in a loft over the living room. Grandma and grandpa would sleep in their 'bedstee' that is a bed much like a hide-a-bed and went into a niche in the living room where behind closed doors it would be hidden from view during the day. The bedstee was raised a few feet with drawers below for the linen and had steps to get into it.

Following are examples of typical bedstees.

In addition to our grandparents, there were a couple of other favorite relatives we would visit. Of course, wherever we went it would be on bicycles. Little Cor would ride with either mom or dad in a little seat they had on the back of their bikes.

Uncle Bram Riedyke and my dad's sister, aunt Jannette (Jan for short), were relatives we loved to visit. Uncle Bram ran a fruit growing business located near the village of Rokanje, at the end of the island next to the North Sea. Huge dunes between his farm and the sea blocked the wind and that protection made for a warmer environment than Holland is generally known for. Uncle Bram had huge glass hothouses in which he grew tomatoes and a variety of fruits. I can still remember the peaches he grew in those hothouses. Their smell was so pungent it was almost overwhelming. To this day if I smell a peach Uncle Bram's farm comes back to me.

Uncle Bram and aunt Jan had a daughter, Jannetje, who was about the same age as me. Jannetje would show us around while the adults visited. She would take us to the dunes and along a path to the beach where we could walk on the warm sand of the beach and explore.

Visiting the Riedykes was probably the longest trip we made on the island. It was a little over twenty miles and took several hours to get there. On the way home we would usually stop at another of my dad's sisters, Neeltje, married to Pete Kerverzee, who owned a dairy farm. They had one son a couple of years older than me. Their farm had a large hay barn next to where they milked cows. We would play in the hayloft where there was a swing on which we could swing out and drop down into a pile of loose hay.

As time went by traveling became restricted due to all the German military activity. Though there was no combat in the immediate area the Germans constructed vast installations such as bunkers and gun emplacements. Since a huge seaport and oil refineries were nearby they felt this was a key location that had to be protected.

German bunkers along the North Sea in the dunnes

We kids were curious about the war and all the activity was fascinating. But with no radio, newspapers or other means of communication we could only guess what was going on based on conversations dad had with his friends.

I had a good friend named Kees Rosmolen who lived on the same road as we did. We were the same age but Kees was a big kid and much taller than we Vander Waals. Kees and I did everything together. We would explore the countryside and, trying to figure out what the Germans were building, sneak into places we should not have been. We scrounged the neighborhood for anything we could use for our own tunnels and mini bunkers that we built into the side of our dyke. Then we would cover everything with wood, soil and sod so they couldn't be seen by anyone. They had secret trap doors and we even made cooking facilities to cook potatoes and carrots, while all the time pretending we were fighting the Germans. Of course, I also had to care for little brother Cor who was always around.

When I was going into the second grade Cor was about five and ready to start kindergarten. But, since he didn't have a bike, yet he would ride on the back of my bike to and from school. In winter snow or when there were high winds, we couldn't ride a bike to school and had to walk. Cor eventually got his own bike. As to the war, everything seemed quite normal to us because we didn't know any different.

Wheat was a rotational crop to potatoes, onions and sugar beets, that were the predominate crops in our area. Before the Germans flooded our area in 1944 I remember picking leftover wheat in fields after farmers harvested the crop and hauled it to threshing machines. My mother was an extremely frugal person and if she could get some free food she was right there to help herself. Prior to a farmer plowing everything under for another crop my mother would ask permission to pick any wheat left on the ground. She would then take Cor and me to hand pick what was left of the wheat by pulling the heads from the stems and putting them in gunnysacks.

Dad would take the wheat we brought home and beat it with a club to loosen the grain, which he would put on a big tarp laying on the ground and toss the chaff into the air to let the wind separate grain from chaff. The clean grain was taken to the big windmill in the village where it was ground into flour. We would usually end up with a couple of sacks of flour mom used for baking.

We also raised rabbits for their fur and meat. It was our job to feed and clean the rabbit cages. There was also a big demand for mole pelts as the fur was great for aviation jackets liners. Mole pelts brought a much higher price than that of rabbit so dad would take my brother Cor and me out mole catching. Soil was very rich in the fields around us and had a lot of worms for moles to feed upon.

It was our job to spot underground mole activity near holes where they would push dirt to the surface. Dad would then sneak up on the unsuspecting mole and with one scoop get the mole out of the ground. The moles were quickly killed and put in a sack. When we had a sack full we would take the moles home where dad would skin them and stretch the hide on a small board with some nails. After a couple of weeks he would remove the stiff hides to take them and some rabbit hides to a fur buyer in the village.

Since we were living close to a train stop Kees suggested one day that we take a little train ride and came up with an idea to sneak on the local steam train. Putting Kees' plan to action we laid in tall grass waiting for the train and when it was stopped to load passengers and cargo we jumped on from the other side. We then sneaked into the cargo portion of a train car and hid behind some boxes while waiting for the train to start moving. The train moved out and when the conductor wasn't looking we came out of hiding and pretended we had paid a fare. However, it didn't take long for the conductor to come back to check for tickets we didn't have. We pleaded that we were only going to the next stop and after a good scolding the conductor let us off at the next stop. Originally, we thought we could catch a train going back the other way but that didn't happen and we had to walk back. It was a long walk home that took hours. My mother was never told about our little train adventure that took place in late 1942 when I was six years old.

The local train – a common mode of transportation

It was not long after our train escapade that Kees suggested we need to do some more exploring and see what the Germans were building on the outer sea dyke. We lived on the Ruigendyke, which was a low interior dyke for one of the polders in the area. It was where grandpa and grandma Vander Waal had a small farm and the large outer sea dyke was only about 8 miles away.

The sea dyke was one of the outer dykes that protected us from the North Sea. It was a huge dyke that stretched from grandpa's farm to Helevoetsluis, a sea port about 25 miles away. The sea dyke was about fifty feet high and very wide. It had huge rocks on the water side and on the earthen back side was grass where local farmers grazed their cattle.

As it faced the sea it made sense the Germans would build military installation near or on top of the sea dyke. At the time we kids didn't know much as to what was really going on with regards to the war but had heard enough from our parents to make us very curious.

It was forbidden to go anywhere near where Germans were building and signs were posted everywhere warning people to keep away. However, that did not deter us as we simply had to see it all for ourselves.

Since it was only about an hour ride by bike, and in an area where there was almost no traffic, we thought we could convince mother to let us go to grandma's for a visit. It took some real talking and she finally agreed, but only if we took little Cor with us. On a nice sunny summer day, after mom told us to please stay out of trouble and look after Cor, we were off to visit grandma. If mom had known what our real plans were we would never gotten out of the house.

We made it to grandma's without any problems and she was really surprised to see the three of us. Grandma made us some hot chocolate and gave us some cookies. We had a nice visit then asked grandma if she would look after Cor while Kees and I did a little exploring near the dyke, Grandma said she would and Kees and I headed off on our bikes to the big dyke.

Sea dyke

On top of the dyke there was a service road that was blocked to keep people from going on it. There was also a lower road that ran near the bottom of the dyke and in normal times this is where traffic traveled. This road was blocked for automobile traffic but we managed to get our bicycles around the barricade and proceed toward the German installations we could see in the distance. As we came closer the construction we saw a series of bunkers near the top of the dyke with big guns that pointed out to sea. Wow! We didn't ride our bikes any further and hid them in some tall grass near the bottom road. Crouching down on our bellies, we sneaked toward the first gun installation, a huge concrete structure with a long gun barrel sticking seaward. It was thrilling to actually see some of the German gun sites we had heard so much about.

We didn't see any soldiers so we continued to creep through the grass to get a better look, assuming they must have been inside having some lunch. It wasn't long before a couple of soldiers came out and stood next to the bunker having a cigarette. Since it was nice and warm they were clearly enjoying a little break in the sun. Kees and I didn't dare move because they were sure to spot us. We just lay there for quite a while waiting for them to go back inside. One solder eventually went back in the structure but the other stayed out and our time was running out. We had to do something because we needed to get back to grandma's before it got too late.

Staying as low as possible in the tall grass we started to crawl away from the bunker when all of a sudden we heard a very loud "HALT!" A soldier carrying a gun had come over to see who we were. Not knowing what to do we decided it better to just stand up and surrender. Fortunately for us once the soldier saw we were a couple of little kids he became more relaxed and asked us what we were doing there. He couldn't speak much Dutch and we couldn't speak German. Neither of us could really understand the other but we were able to convince him we were just a couple of curious kids who wanted to see what was built on the dyke.

The soldier must of felt sorry for us and probably didn't want to go through reporting procedures with his superiors so he told us to immediately get out of the area, not to come back. Man, you should have seen us run down to the lower road next to the dyke and back towards where we had hidden our bikes. I don't think my legs ever moved any faster as when we made that exit. When we got back to grandma's house we didn't dare, say a word about what we saw or did. We picked up Cor and made our way home, thinking how close we had come to getting into some real trouble. Or worse, possibly being shot. That was a harrowing close encounter with the German army and we were happy, or should I say very relieved, it ended as it did

Chapter III – THE MOVE FROM OUR FIRST HOME

In 1943 mom and dad were informed we had to move out of our rented house. The owner of the house had a son who was getting married and needed the house. It was not an easy time as no house building was allowed because the Germans were using all construction materials. Consequently, there was a housing shortage. However, with a lot of help from relatives and friends, dad found a little house on the other side of town on the Molendyke. This was a big change for dad because up until this time he was able to either walk to work or ride his bike. Now he was about ten miles from his job and that meant getting up an hour earlier and a lot of pedaling his bike to work. Our new address on the Molendyke must have come from the big windmill located near town next to the dyke. The windmill had been there hundreds of years and used to grind grain. After our move from the Ruigendyk to the Molendyke, we started to understand the war a little better --- probably because we were growing up and getting a little bit wiser.

Oudenhoorn, Molendijk

The Van Henniks' business employed dad to haul potatoes into the city for a distributor who then resold them to local stores. Dad worked long hours but potatoes are the number one staple in Holland and his job was critical to getting produce into the city. Unfortunately, during the war there wasn't much money around and what there was had little or no value. People from the city would come to the farms and use jewelry, silverware, gold, small radios or almost anything of worth that could be used to barter for food. The Van Henniks did very well because, in addition to selling potatoes, they did a lot of bartering for goods that could be later sold for profit. They were much like many farmers in the area who also made a lot of money.

Dad always made sure our family had food on the table and he too bartered in a small way by using a few extra sacks of potatoes, and sometimes sugar beets, he put on the truck early in the morning before he left for the city. Sugar beets were plentiful in our area but generally used to process sugar and not eaten. However, since food was scarce city people would cook them just like potatoes.

Sugar beet

Using his 'trading stock' dad would often bring home special treats and foods we couldn't get at our local store. Sometimes dad would really surprise us with some unusual things he picked up bartering. One day he came home with a big surprise wrapped up in some old towels. As we kids were really into war fantasies dad knew we would surely like what he brought home and couldn't wait to show us. When the surprise was unwrapped it turned out to be a small automatic machine gun something like a British Sten gun. It had a short barrel with a wire stock and probably something used by German paratroopers when they first invaded Holland. Wow! We couldn't believe our eyes or that dad would actually trade potatoes for a gun. We were ecstatic to see and touch a real German gun. The gun didn't have the long ammo magazine that sticks out the bottom and with that missing it was harmless. Even so, dad knew we would be excited just to see something like that.

Sten gun

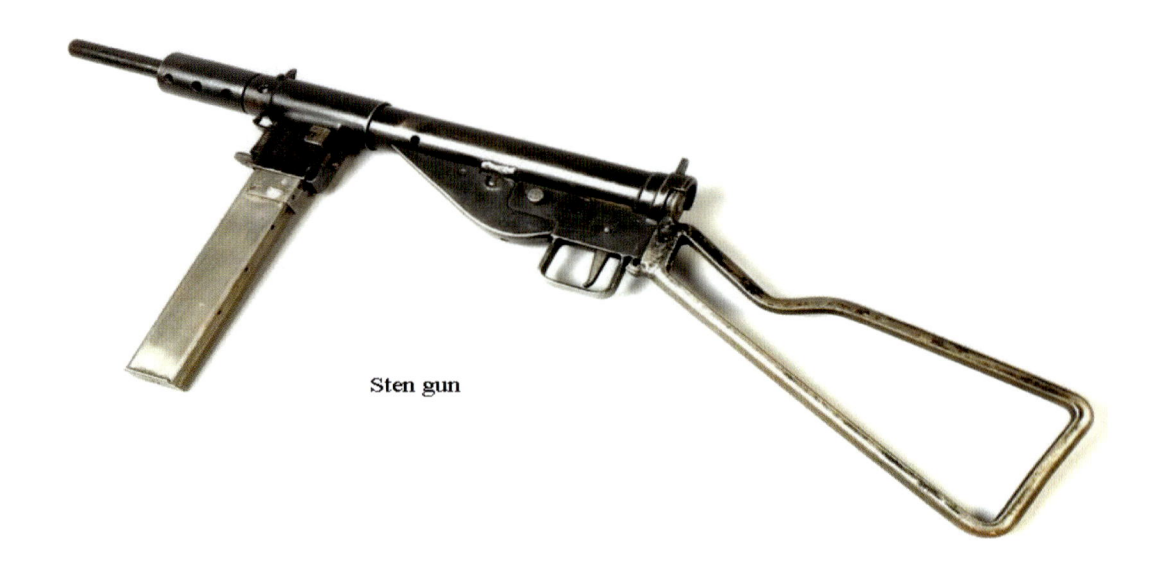

Bringing home the gun did not go over very well with my mother. Mom immediately told dad she did not want that thing in the house and to get rid of it. That night, while he thought we were sleeping, dad went outside to bury the gun. He dug a hole at the end of our garden near the pigpen and placed it in the ground.

Having heard dad go outdoors after mom's orders Cor and I figured he must have buried the gun to make her happy. When dad went to work the next morning we went looking for the gun. It didn't take us long to find it. Making sure mom wasn't watching we dug up the gun and put the hole back like when we found it. We cleaned the gun then hid it in our shed near where we kept rabbits. At that age, just holding a real gun gave us a tremendous thrill but we had to be very careful not to let mom know we had it.

It wasn't long before our friends found out we had a German trophy. Being ever so proud, we had to show the gun around to let them actually see and touch it. That made us quite popular in our circle of friends. Eventually the gun disappeared. We were not sure if dad found it or it got stolen but we surely couldn't say anything to either dad or mom.

In retrospect, it was probably a good thing we didn't have the gun any longer because we could have gotten into a lot of trouble. If word got out in the village and the wrong people heard about it my dad would have had real difficulty trying to explain how he came by that gun. There was never any discussion as to what might have happened to the gun and it was never seen again.

In the fall of 1943 our family rode our bikes to visit Uncle Bram at his vegetable farm in Rokanje. On the way we came across a strange site I didn't understand at the time. A group of local people and German soldiers were cutting down all the trees that lined the road. There were also teams of horses that pulled the tree trunks into the fields where they were planted in holes that had been dug about every couple of hundred feet apart. I asked dad why were they doing that but at the time he didn't know and said he would try to find out.

At a later time dad found out why all those tree trunks were put out in the field. The Germans were expecting an invasion from England to come into our area. Poles and tree trunks were to stop gliders filled with soldiers and jeeps from being able to land in flat fields. As it turned out the invasion never came and instead planned for the French coast at Normandy, about eight months later in June of 1944. There the Germans did not have the poles in the fields like in Holland but the gliders faced another problem just as dangerous. The French countryside behind German lines had fields crisscrossed with hedgerows to divide them. The hedgerows consisted of trees, shrubs and other vegetation that covered rows of rocks that made barrier that did not look like it would be of much resistance. Gliders that landed in those fields would run into the hedgerows and it was a disaster for the glider and its contents --- mostly Allied solders who suffered many casualties. Gliders were towed by a tow plane and released over the intended landing zone. Sadly, once a glider is cut loose from its tow plane it has to land somewhere and those crisscrossed fields were the planned landing sites.

Logs and poles placed upright in the fields to cause damage to gliders was called **Rommelspargel** (Rommel's asparagus), named after Field Marshal Irwin Rommel who ordered their design and usage. Rommel himself called the defensive tactic **Luftlandehindernis** (air landing obstacle).

Many World War II gliders were the Waco model CG4's, built in the United States then shipped to England in kit form and assembled just before flight. Over 13,000 gliders were built and most of them only used for just one flight --- as was planned.

The **Waco CG-4A** was the most widely used United States troop/cargo military glider of World War II. It was designated the **CG-4A** by the United States Army Air Forces,[1] and named **Hadrian** in British military service.

Designed by the Waco Aircraft Company, flight testing began in May 1942, and eventually more than 13,900 CG-4As were delivered.

CG-4A

Role	Military glider
Manufacturer	Waco Aircraft Company
First flight	1942
Primary users	United States Army Air Forces
	Royal Air Force
	Royal Canadian Air Force
	United States Navy
Number built	>13,903

In addition to glider problems playing a deadly role at Normandy, bad weather and beaches completely controlled by huge German gun emplacements also caused massive Allied forces casualties.

Crashed glider landing at Normandy

Upon our arrival at Uncle Bram's place in Rokanja, mom and dad visited over afternoon tea. In the meantime, I started talking to their daughter Janetje who is my age and reminded her of the trouble we almost got into with our adventure of sneaking up on the German installation on the sea dyke. Janetje then told me about all sorts of bunkers and towers the Germans built on our dunes, probably to guard the entrance to the Maas River and Port of Rotterdam. She said she knew of a secret way to get closer to the installations for a good look. We were all game for that and she proceeded to lead us through the dunes to where there was a barrier fence with all sorts of barbed wire and signs to stay out. She also said she knew a place where we could crawl under the fence through the sand and should not get spotted. Curious as we were the temptation was just too great for us not to do it.

Following Janetje's lead, we slid under the fence and started to sneak up closer to the bunker installations, keeping down real low so as not to get caught. As we sneaked closer and closer to the bunkers, we suddenly heard in the distance some sort of motor vehicle that seemed to be coming nearer to where we were hiding. We also heard a barking dog and realized we must have been spotted by one of the watchtowers. Quickly, we made a run back to where we came under the fence. It was none too soon for in looking back we saw a jeep with two guards and a German Shepard dog coming toward the hole in the fence we had just made it through. Fortunately, they couldn't pursue us because there was no way for them to get on our side of the fence. We ran like hell back to Uncle Bram's place and pretended like nothing had happened.

After returning from our little adventure mom and dad soon finished their visit so we helped them gather some fruit and vegetables to take home. Uncle Bram always had good things for us to take home because he had huge glass hothouses where he grew vegetables and fruit we couldn't grow where we lived.

Another interesting recollection is of big concrete barges tied up in the Voornse Canal near where my grandmother lived. Early in the war the Germans had planned to catch the British off guard and invade England. A large fleet of ships, tugs and barges had been gathered for the invasion but some smart thinking Germans prevailed and the invasion was called off. I believe it might have been because low free board barges being towed in bad weather would have made the fleet sitting ducks for British aircraft and England's shore batteries. The planned German invasion was named 'Operation Sea Lion' and an overly ambitious idea. I have the book that details how that invasion was conceived and to be carried out.

Operation Sea Lion barges on Voornse Canal near grandma Snoek's house

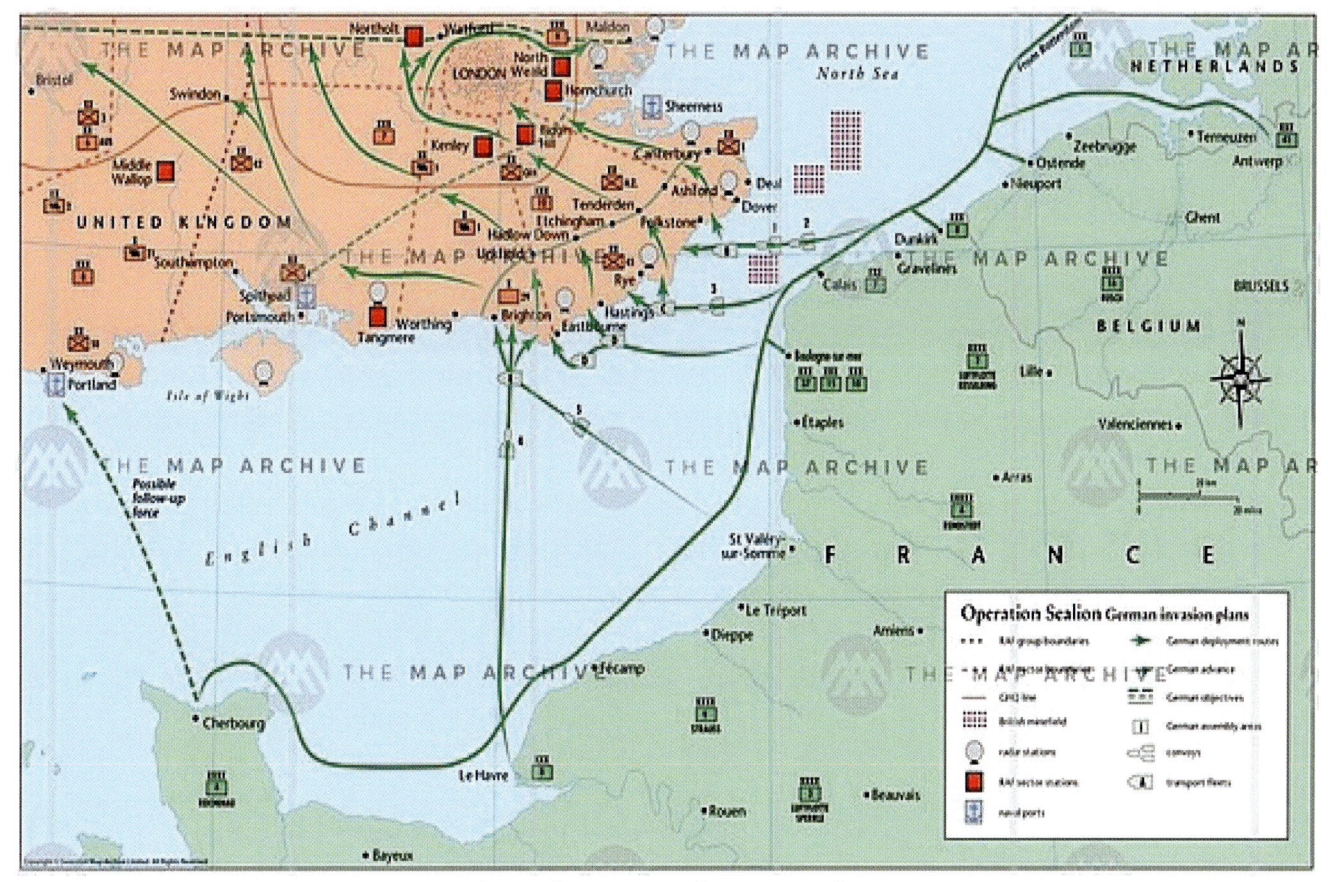

Plans for Operation Sea Lion

A major impact upon the Dutch during the occupation was what Germans called ***ARBEITSEINSATE***, a program that forced every man between the ages of 18 to 45 to register for work in German war production factories. Approximately 500,000 Dutchmen were rounded up and transported by force to Germany. A large number of Dutchmen resisted the round up because they knew that it would be almost certain death by starvation, forced labor or relentless Allied bombing of German factories. Many tried to hide out or would join the Dutch Resistance, which was almost as dangerous for if caught they would certainly be shot. And, when men were found in hiding, an additional ten people in the area where they were caught would be shot. Germans did this to discourage people from hiding those who would not go to work in Germany. This also was done when people would hide Allied pilots who parachuted after being shot down over Holland.

Some of our relatives endured that program and survived. I later found out upon visiting my cousin Corrie that her husband was one of those 'taken' young men and had a lot of stories on how close he came to being killed by the Allied bombings. One in particular among the young men who refused to go to Germany to work was Han Mastenbroek who later married my dad's niece, Neeltje. You will read more about Han later.

The Dutch resistance played a very important role in slowing down the German invasion. It was well organized and consisted of many Dutch ex-military in hiding. The resistance did a lot of damage to German installations and truck convoys. They were also helpful in hiding downed Allied airmen.

Then there was the ongoing search for Jewish families the Germans called 'Jude'. When found they had to wear a yellow Star of David on the outside of their clothing. Most of the Jewish who had money had already left the country before the war. Those who didn't were using the 'underground' to smuggle them out of the country. The Dutch resistance also hid people sought after by the German police and called 'under divers'. Most were Dutch Jews who chose to 'dive under' because they were banished from public life by the Germans after their shops were confiscated and evicted from their homes. Jews who weren't able to get out of the country were rounded up and shipped to German concentration camps then later to 'death camps'. The Germans killed over one million Jews from Holland alone. Also during the war over 140,000 Dutch people died of starvation or as resistance fighters.

By 1943 hostility between the Dutch and occupying forces was on the rise. Tension was further exacerbated by German construction of the *Atlantic Wall,* a massive project built for coastal defense. It was a line that started in southern France, ran through Belgium and Holland, then on to Denmark and Norway. The defenses consisted primarily of bunkers and gun emplacements built on dunes along the coastal shore. Thousands of homes in the path of construction were demolished and the many, many occupants displaced.

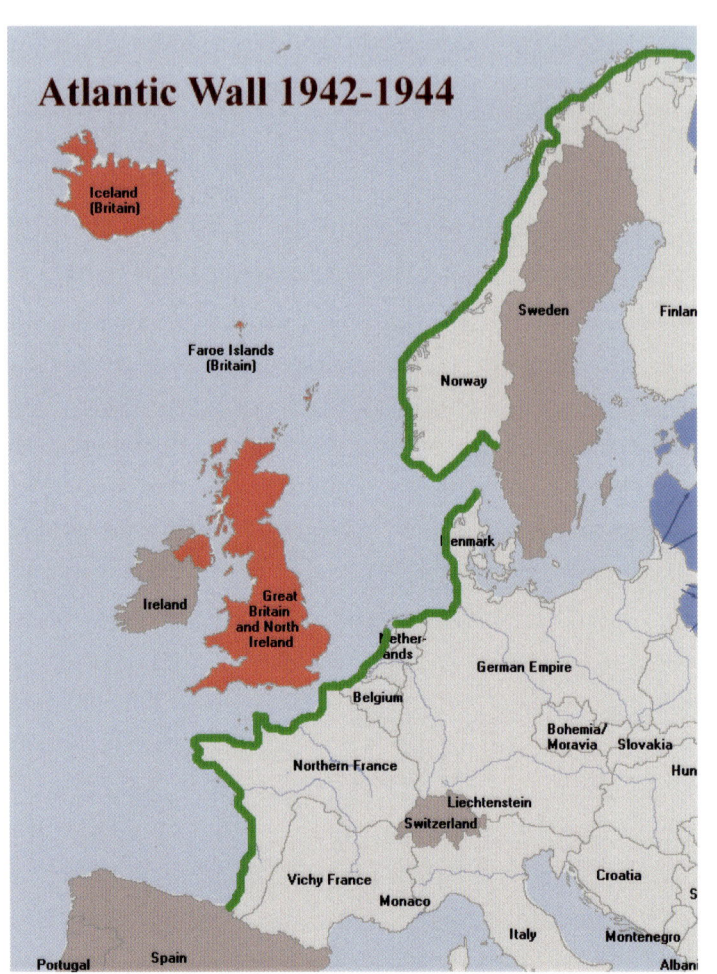

Hitler ordered the construction of the Atlantic Wall fortifications in 1942 through his Fuhrer Directive No. 40.

More than half a million French workers were drafted (forced) to build it. The wall was frequently mentioned in Nazi propaganda where its size and strength were usually exaggerated.

Thousands of German troops were stationed in its defenses. Today, ruins of the wall exist in all of the nations where it was built, although many structures have fallen into the ocean or have been demolished over the years.

Today you can visit the ruins of bunkers and emplacements throughout Holland, left as a lasting reminder of the German occupation.

Atlantic Wall construction

Forced labor constructing wall

Atlantic Wall gun emplacement

Chapter IV – OUR VILLAGE AND THE FLOODING OF THE POLDERS

We had been living on the Molendyke for about a year when ordered to leave our home because the polders in that area were to be flooded. The Germans were going to breach the outer dykes as a way to prevent what they believed would be an invasion by Allied forces. With only a couple of weeks notice we packed our belongings and put furniture upstairs because everything downstairs would be under water. Dad set out to find us another place to live.

NOTE: INFO BELOW FROM GERMAN RECORDS

It was good to be part of a large family because when dad contacted his sister, Aunt Kriss, a place to live was found. Aunt Kriss was married to a man who owned a small grocery store located just off the town square in the village of Abbenbroek. They had no bedrooms available but until suitable housing was found we could live upstairs over their store where inventory was kept. By rearranging boxes of goods and big rounds of cheese we made ourselves enough room to sleep at night. To this day I can still remember the strong smell of that well aged cheese.

Living in Abbenbroek meant we had to start a new school again and make new friends. One of those friends was Henk, a boy a little older, taller than us and even more adventuresome than we were. It didn't take long before we became good buddies and a band of kids always looking for war activities, souvenirs and anything or everything the Germans were doing.

Cor and I did not need to ride our bicycles to go to school when living with Aunt Kriss. It was a small village and only about a block to the far end of the town square. Our school was close to the church and community hall located in that area. There was a road that made a loop around a pond in the middle of the town and on that road were storefronts and homes. In the middle of the pond a covered bandstand sat on pilings. Later, when the Canadians liberated Holland, food distribution took place near the town hall.

Town square

We only stayed at Aunt Kriss' for about a month when dad made alternative living arrangements with an old friend, Leen Byle, who owned a trucking company a half-mile away. Leen was a bachelor and lived with a housekeeper. His house was on the main road leading into Abbenbroek and, since it was such a large place, we could live there. Leen and his housekeeper would live in the back part of the house and we would live in the front. There was a loft above the living room with plenty of room for all of us to sleep. This was a major improvement over sleeping with cheese in Aunt Kriss' store. However, dad was now further from his work. Since the land had been flooded there wasn't much work available but dad was able to support us by doing part-time jobs on Leen's property and driving his trucks.

While living in Leen's house 'non-professional' German soldiers were sent in to replace experienced soldiers needed on front lines. The replacements were draftees who were not really interested in the war and just putting in time. They were taking real advantage of the local people, as to food, liquor and women, however. One day some German officers came to look over Leen's big house and discovered we were also living there. They wanted to commandeer the house but, fortunately, the issue was settled amicably as they only wanted our living quarters during the day and the house would be ours at night.

Being on a main road we kids were enthralled with watching something happening all the time. Lots of soldiers and convoys of military equipment were always being moved to different parts of the island. Along the road Germans had dug foxholes about ten feet long, six feet deep, three feet wide and spaced about every one hundred feet. They were made for the protection of convoy crews and soldiers on the trucks. When convoys were strafed by Allied planes the soldiers would leave their vehicles and jump into a nearby foxhole.

The foxholes were not without 'side effects'. When first dug we kids would play in them. However, that didn't last long because city dwellers that came to barter for food found them a great place to use as a toilet. That sure put a stop to our playing in the foxholes. Another pitfall was that German soldiers who were returning from town after a night of drinking often fell into their own foxholes.

During 1944 and 1945 electricity was usually cut off during the night. The Germans did not want lights showing anywhere and we had to have blackout curtains on our windows. Consequently, we came up with all sorts of gadgets that gave a bit of light at night. Dad rigged up a bicycle with a generator that provided some light as long someone was pedaling but it really wasn't the answer. The most effective method for lighting was a kerosene float light. It was simply a quart jar filled partially with water. Kerosene was then added and a little wooden float with a wick put on top. These would last all night and emit about the same amount of light as a candle. Mom cooked on kerosene stoves that only had a single burner, which meant she had to use a couple of them to make a meal. The stoves were small, did not take up much room and easily stored when finished cooking.

The only bad thing about using kerosene was that it was dirty and the house with everything in it smelled like kerosene.

Mini Kerosene Stoves mom used during the war at Leen Byl s house

A typical kerosene float light using a cork and wick

While the new occupation troops were easier to get along with they did give us problems. Stealing food was one big issue and if we didn't hide everything edible it would just disappear. I remember that mom had a ham hanging in the cellar that she planned to use throughout the winter. One day she discovered it was gone and by candle drippings she knew who took it. German soldiers! Mom was not one you wanted to cross and she was mad. She immediately went to the commander of the local troops to express her displeasure and, though she didn't get her ham back, they did give her food to replace it. I believe mom would have been shot if that commander had been one of the 'regular' German army.

Another incident I recall was the infamous 'clothing caper'. Dutch people are known for their cleanliness. German soldiers in our area, not so much. After mom did laundry she would put clean underwear in a chest of drawers in the hallway. One day some German officers decided they needed a change of clothing and purloined our underwear. When mom later went to get clean clothes from the drawers she found a bunch of dirty German underwear. Wow, was she upset! She again went off on the officers in charge but they just laughed at her. That did it! Mom didn't want to touch their 'stuff' so she got a stick, piled it all in a stack outside and lit fire to it. Again, if dealing with the regular German army, mom's little stunt would have been a death sentence but these guys didn't seem to give a hoot.

Our home was fairly close to the seacoast where German fighter planes guarded against incoming Allied bombers. Fighter planes escorted Allied bombers as they came from England and when German fighter planes flew up to intercept bombers dogfights took place in the skies above us.

USAAF B-17 on bombing run to Germany

Quite often we would lie on our backs on the side of our local dyke and watch the dogfights. They usually lasted about half an hour then the planes left the area, probably to refuel. Allied fighters flew back to England and German fighters back to airfields in either Germany or Holland. Dogfights were always a good show but it was difficult to see who was shot down --- a German fighter or an Allied fighter --- until they fell low enough to make out the insignia.

Dogfight: German Folke Wolfe – USAAF P 51 Mustang

Dogfight: RAF Spitfire MK IX - German Messerschmitt BF 109g

Dogfights provided us a lot of excitement but I'm not sure that as children our minds quite grasped the full meaning of "life or death" situations those airmen were in. About half of the time a plane got shot down a pilot or crewmember would bail out. At the crash site of a plane or where downed airmen would land, depending if it was a German or Allied, the area was usually shut down and we could not have access to the wreck. Dogfights were almost a daily event when the weather was good and we saw many planes come crashing down.

One of our group heard of a plane that came down in a pasture near our area and knew the proximate location. Our little band quickly set out to find the plane and after a couple hours of looking we spotted the crash site. However, it was definitely not what we expected. The plane evidently nose-dived straight into the pasture where it was flat and soft. And it must have hit with tremendous force because there wasn't any plane to see at all. There was only a big crater about six feet deep with the plane buried somewhere deep in the ground. We only found a few small pieces of aluminum and Plexiglas. That was it. Wow! What a disappointment! We dug around in the hole to see if we could retrieve anything more than the few pieces we found lying about or if there was anything to see of the plane. No luck. Maybe the larger pieces were picked up by the military but we never did find out.

Site of plane crash

Back home we went to get ready for our next search mission and it wasn't long before we heard of another downed plane. Off we rode on our bikes and discovered it was a German plane that tried to land on the road and ended up crashing into a house. The plane was really badly damaged and we didn't see or know if the pilot made it out. There were no guards posted at the crash site, probably because the plane was so badly mangled, but we were able to see the plane up close. We even managed to get a few souvenirs to take home.

German planes crashed into houses

We lived about ten miles from a V1 launching site. These were the 'buzz bombs' Germany had as one of its secret weapons and doing a lot of damage in England. V1's had ramjet engines with shutters at the intake that caused their strange and distinctive buzzing sound. Buzz bombs engines would not work without airflow so rockets were used to boost them into the air. They had a big failure rate because after the launch the engine simply would not start. Most buzz bombs were launched at night from a trailer and we would lie in bed to listen for their sound. As long as there was sound everything would be OK around us. When there was no sound after launch we knew there was going to be a crash and the bomb would come down anywhere in the direction of England. We lost relatives and friends due to V1's crashing into their homes.

V-1 Mobile launch

V-1 Fixed launch site

V-1 flying bomb
Fieseler Fi 103
Flakzielgerät 76 (FZG-76)

The V-1 was designed under the codename *Kirschkern* (cherry stone)[8] by Lusser and Gosslau, with a fuselage constructed mainly of welded sheet steel and wings built of plywood. The simple, Argus-built pulse jet engine pulsed 50 times per second,[2] and the characteristic buzzing sound gave rise to the colloquial names "buzz bomb" or "doodlebug" (a common name for a wide variety of insects). It was known briefly in Germany (on Hitler's orders) as *Maikäfer* (May bug) and *Krähe* (crow).[9]

V-1 cutaway

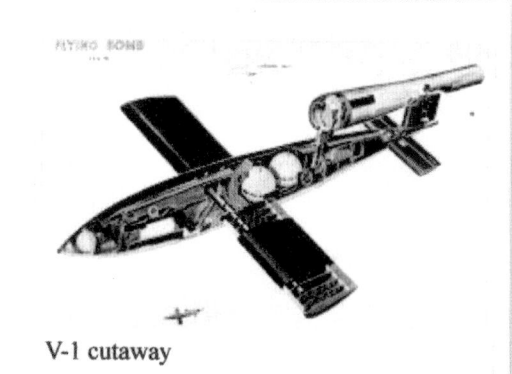

Power plant

Main article: Argus As 014

Ignition of the Argus pulse jet was accomplished using an automotive type spark plug located about 2.5 ft (0.76 m) behind the intake shutters, with current supplied from a portable starting unit. Three air nozzles in the front of the pulse jet were at the same time connected to an external high pressure air source which was used to start the engine. Acetylene gas was typically used for starting, and very often a panel of wood or similar material was held across the end of the tailpipe to prevent the fuel from diffusing and escaping before ignition. The V-1 was fueled by 150 gallons of 75 octane gasoline.

Once the engine had been started and the temperature had risen to the minimum operating level, the external air hose and connectors were removed and the engine's resonant design kept it firing without any further need for the electrical ignition system, which was used only to ignite the engine when starting.

It is a common myth that the V-1's Argus As 014 pulse jet engine needed a minimum airspeed of 150 mph (240 km/h) to operate. The Argus As 014 (also known as a resonant jet) could in fact operate at zero airspeed due to the nature of its intake shutters and its acoustically tuned resonant combustion chamber. Contemporary film footage of the V-1 always shows the distinctive pulsating exhaust of a fully running engine before the catapult system is triggered and the missile launched.[citation needed] The origin of this myth may lie in the fact that due to the low static thrust of the pulse jet engine and the very high stall speed of the small wings, the V-1 could not take off under its own power in a practically short distance, and thus required to either be launched by aircraft catapult or be airlaunched from a modified bomber aircraft such as the Heinkel He-111. Ground-launched V-1s were typically propelled up an inclined launch ramp by an apparatus known as a *Dampferzeuger* ("steam generator")

The V1 was not a fast flying bomb and that is one reason they were launched at night. After the lower part of Holland near the Belgium border was liberated the Allies would try to shoot down the V1's using searchlights and tracer bullets. We were close enough to actually see the tracer bullets in the distance. In daytime British fighter planes could catch up with a V1 to tip its wing and send it into a different direction. It is thought that if V1's had been introduced earlier the tide of the war could have changed for in the short time they were in use they did a massive amount of damage to London.

I recall going with dad to where a V1 rocket crashed into a relative's house. There wasn't much left of their house and because the V1 was launched at night both people living there were killed while sleeping.

Home destroyed by errant V1

The V1 was launched from trailers or land based sites. About 20,000 V1s were launched toward London with over 20% failing right after launch. We were living on the edge of a V1 flight path and many crashed around our countryside. The one that crashed into our relative's house was only about ten miles from its launch site.

When our friend Henk found out we had visited the house where a V1 crashed he got all excited and wanted us to join him in seeing how close we could get a German launch site.

V1s were reportedly launched from the village of Spykenisse, which was not that far from our house. We figured it would take about an hour to get there on our bikes so one day we set out to find the sites. Our ride took us to a huge industrial area of sugar beet processing plants, oil refineries and all sorts of heavy industry. It was also where a big bridge crossed the Maas River and a lot of activity and traffic was taking place. Check points were everywhere and we were soon stopped by German sentries. Fearing the consequences, we abandoned the idea of trying to find the V1 launch sites and went back home. *In later doing research I learned that V1 launch sites were set up amid the large sugar beet processing plants that we saw. It was a perfect place to set up launch trailers and not get spotted from the air by Allied planes.*

On D-Day, June 6, 1944, with the largest amphibian forces ever assembled, Allied forces came ashore on Normandy beaches in France. The Dutch people believed the war would be over in a matter of months as the Germans surrendered Paris to the Allies on August 24th then in September, Brussels in Belgium. The Dutch thought the Allies were right on the doorsteps of Holland. Antwerp was next -- right on the border of Belgium and Holland -- and Dutch people were already starting to celebrate the arrival of Allied troops. But that didn't happen. Unbelievable fighting took place between the Allies and Germans in the southern parts of Holland and lasted until the end of 1944. The Allies were stopped at the Rhine River and lost a major battle at Arnhem. It was called 'Operation Market Garden' and a huge failure for the Allies.

OPERATION MARKET-GARDEN 1944

Parachutes and gliders during operation Market Garden 1944

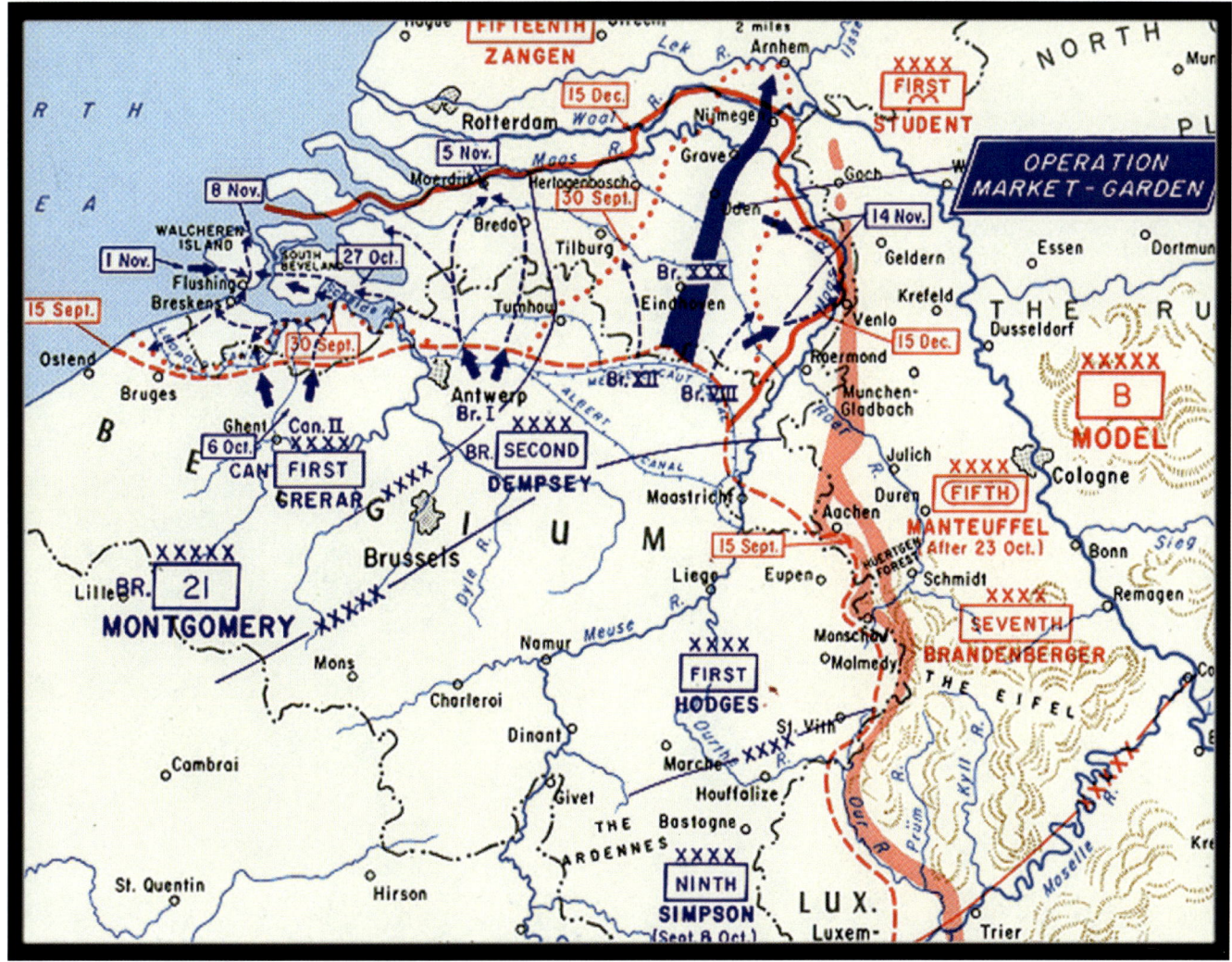

Operation Market Garden Battle Plan

Operation Market Garden took place from September 17th to September 25th. 1944, and was the largest airborne operation of World War II. British and US troops used gliders and a massive parachute drop to land behind the German lines. Sadly, many were ambushed in the fields and surrounded by Germans. There were a horrendous number of Allied casualties.

The Allies' plan was to create a sixty-mile corridor that lead into Germany. There was a series of nine bridges that needed to be captured in order for the Allies to cross the rivers Rhine and Waal. However, the Germans blew up most of them before they were captured. Only one bridge at the town of Remagen remained and Allied forces rushed to capture it before it too was demolished. A major battle ensued with over 15,000 Allied soldiers killed.

The movie 'A Bridge Too Far' --- with an all-star cast --- affords a realistic version of that battle.

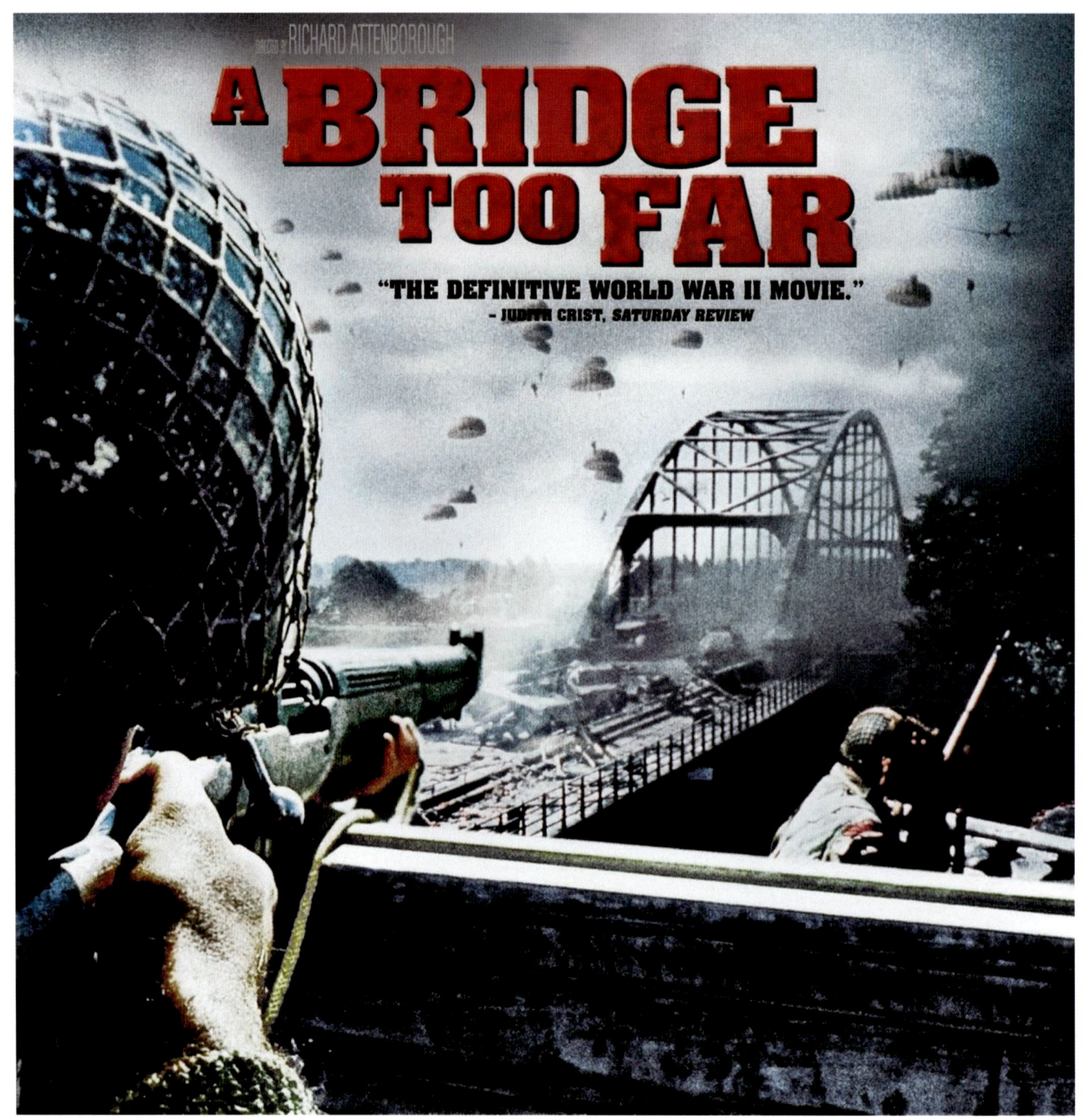

A BRIDGE TOO FAR movie poster

The Allies also recommended a railroad strike by the Dutch who operated trains between Holland and Germany. Trains that hauled food, supplies, and particularly, coal for power plants. Their thinking was if trains were stopped it would help the war effort because Germany would be denied supplies needed to continue the war. Subsequently, trainmen walked off their jobs and went into hiding. Little did they know the plan failed, yet the strike lasted another eight months. No trains running meant power stations could not supply electricity for homes and, worse, the Dutch primarily used coal for heat.

The winter of 1944-1945 was an extremely cold winter and became known as the *Dutch Hunger Winter* due to famine that touched all who were living in the cities. The Dutch railroad strike already halted the fuel supply then the Germans stopped food going into the cities from farm towns. People were starving and freezing to death. It was truly a miserable time.

The *Dutch Hunger Winter* affected some 4.5 million people. Soup kitchens with soup lines were set up throughout the cities to provide a minimum meal for those who could get to them. It is estimated that over 18,000 people became victim to the famine and it was reported most were elderly men. The famine lasted until the end of the war in May 1945, when Allied planes and trucks brought food to the cities again.

Hongerwinter – the Dutch famine 1944-5

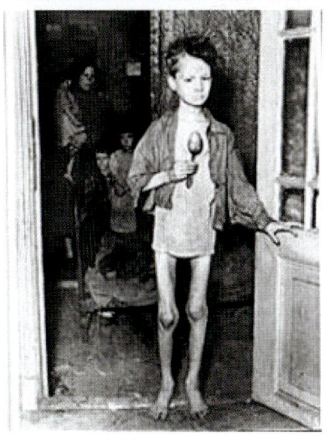

During that winter we were still living in Leen Byles' house and though dad could not haul potatoes into the city Leen had other work for him. Between that and dad being well connected with many local farmers our family was never without food.

Leen Byle's place had a large yard for parking his trucks and the Germans took advantage of it to park many of their trucks and equipment. It was quite an assortment of vehicles as there were also smaller jeeps and trailers. Some of the larger trucks had canvas covers, probably for hauling supplies or soldiers. One day, among that equipment, we found a rubber-tired wagon that was to be pulled by horses and it was just sitting there smelling really sour.

German Army field ovens

That particular wagon was piled high with fresh bread, which meant there must have been a field kitchen nearby where it was baked. Though we loved bread, we were curious about that strange odor and just had to get a few loaves so we could actually taste it.

Hampering our plan to get to the bread was that a guard was usually on duty watching over the parked vehicles. To accomplish our goal we had to hide next to the house and wait for the guard to take a break. When the guard finally did leave a couple of us sneaked into the yard, climbed up on the bread wagon and tossed down a couple of loaves to the others. Having gained our prize, we took the pilfered bread back into the house and cut off a few slices for the ultimate taste test. YUCK! It had a strong vinegar taste and was awful, even with adding some cheese. For bread that looked so good it was simply not edible.

Later we found out that vinegar was used to preserve the bread so it wouldn't quickly go stale. German soldiers must have acquired a taste for that awful tasting sour bread but we couldn't imagine how. We wound up giving the bread to horses kept in a pen next to the truck yard. Even the horses were not keen on eating the bread but eventually ate it. Probably because they were hungry. *NOTE: Horses were used extensively throughout the war because they didn't need gasoline that was extremely in short supply. Many thousands of horses were used to pull light loads and move men and equipment --- and many died.*

While living at Leen Byles' house we kids did a lot of crazy things. It was probably the time I did the most venturesome things in life, that is until my adult years. Our band of kids was all about nine years old and could do things the Germans would never suspect. After all, we were just a bunch of children. By then, however, we had become old enough to know what was going on with regard to the war but still had no fear.

One day we dreamed up the idea that a great war souvenir, and what we all wanted, would be a real German pistol like the officers wore. The problem was that unlike readily available rifles, pistols were a personal item to an officer and of which they were extremely possessive. Nonetheless, we just had to figure out how we could get our hands on one of them. The officers who partied at our house would become immediately suspect if their pistol went missing and that could mean real trouble for my parents. They hated the Germans and would be first to be blamed.

German Lugar pistol

We spent a lot of time thinking on ways we could get access to a pistol. Weeks went by then one day we heard from a friend who was cordial with the Germans that an officer was missing. This was no real surprise because there was always a lot of drinking going on, especially among the officers. Who knows where one could have wound up? To protect Germans from the Dutch Resistance a curfew did not allow civilians to be out after 8:00 PM and when we heard a jeep went missing the same night as the officer, we had a clue.

Our little group had some good ideas about what might of happened to the jeep so we organized a search party to see where it could have ended up. After several days of looking we spotted at a curve on one of the back roads next to a canal what looked like tire tracks that left the road and went right into the canal. However, the water was too murky to see anything so we poked around in it with a long pole. Sure enough, there was something in the water. We suspected it might be the jeep so we cleaned up the tire tracks leading into the water so others couldn't see them. Whoever driving must have been moving really fast because tracks went straight into the canal and the jeep going airborne.

We left the site and did not mention what we found to anyone. After waiting a few days to see if anyone else spotted anything we all took fishing poles and went back to the site pretending we were fishing. Henk, one of the bigger kids, volunteered to dive into the water and take a closer look. When Henk surfaced he said the jeep was there all right and sort of upside down with a dead officer in it. We figured the officer was probably drunk and going way too fast when he came upon the curve then drove into the water. Henk dove in again and came up with the officer's pistol but left everything else in place. Wow! What a find! We hightailed out of there really fast and went on home for a better look at our prize. Henk claimed the pistol for himself because he was the one who dove in the water and retrieved it from the dead officer. But, at least, all of us were able to hold and admire our trophy. We never told anyone what we found, and where. About a week later someone else spotted where the jeep left the road and notified the Germans.

During the latter part of the war we were extremely restricted as to going anywhere. My mother had a sister, Marie, who was twelve years younger than mom and in her early twenties. Since there weren't any young Dutchman around -- they were either working in factories in Germany or hiding -- it was common for young Dutch girls to mingle with German occupation troops. Marie did what many young Dutch girls did. After all, these guys were not exactly the German fighting soldiers and they were available. These soldiers were young draftees, only there to put in their time. And have a good time, it would seem. Marie became pregnant and had a little girl but there was never a marriage as when the war ended the soldiers left. After the war girls like Marie paid a price for their 'fun'. Local townspeople shaved off all the girls' hair so that as a reminder of what they did they would have to walk around bald.

Early in May of 1945 German occupation forces got word the war was coming to an end and the officers who had been using our house decided to celebrate by having an 'end of war' party. As they proceeded to get really drunk things got out of control and they thought a little fun would be shooting out the ceiling lights. Clearly, they were not thinking about us sleeping in the loft above the living room and we were lucky none of their bullets hit us. Dad immediately charged downstairs and confronted the soldiers, telling them in no uncertain terms that we were sleeping right above the living room. It surely must have got their attention because they stopped shooting up the place. During the entire war that was probably the closest we actually came to being in the line of fire.

After the *DUTCH HUNGER WINTER* the end of the war was near but because the Germans had stopped all food transportation people were still starving in the cities. In some way a crazy plan surfaced to have Allied planes drop food into the cities and, amazingly, it was agreed to by the Germans --- somewhat. The plan was called *OPERATION CHOW HOUND* and allowed Allied planes to airlift and drop food to 3.5 million starving Dutch people in the still occupied Holland.

Over 2000 military flights took place between May 1 and May 8, 1945. It must have taken raw courage to fly *OPERATION CHOW HOUND* because American and British aircrews never knew when Luftwaffe fighters would jump them or Germans antiaircraft guns open fire. And flying at only 400 ft above the ground, just clearing treetops, meant the airmen would not have a chance to bail out if their plane was hit. However, over that eight-day period the 120,000 German occupation troops kept their word and never fired on Allied bombers. As the Allied planes flew overhead aircrews saw that Dutch civilians had spelled out huge signs in the tulip fields saying "Thanks Boys". The many Americans who flew *OPERATION CHOW HOUND* would claim that was the best thing they did during the war.

About 1000 'sorties' were flown during *OPERATION CHOW HOUND* with the British flying their Lancaster bombers and US aircrews the B17. These were not cargo planes and the only way they could drop food was by stacking it in the bomb bays of the planes then dropping the loads just like bombs --- but at a very low altitude.

** As a footnote to this historic information I did not find out about *OPERATION CHOW HOUND* until doing research for this book. I then remembered that near the end of the war bombers would come over by the hundreds, flying at treetop level. Their normal pattern was to fly low as they came across the English Channel to stay under German radar and usually had fighter escorts. But during that first week in May there were no fighter escorts and bombers never before flew that low. Sometimes those bombers were flying so low we could even see faces of the pilots and they often waved back at us. This was something completely different and we always wondered why. Being as there was no radio, TV or newspapers to tell the rest of Holland what was going on those of us in the country were not aware of the food drop. *OPERATION CHOW HOUND* dropped food where more people were starving the most, near the big cities of Amsterdam, Rotterdam and Den Haag.

Above: USAAF B17 bomber making a food drop during OPERATION CHOW HOUND

Following page: A British RAF Lancaster bomber making a food drop as grateful Dutch citizens gather and wave

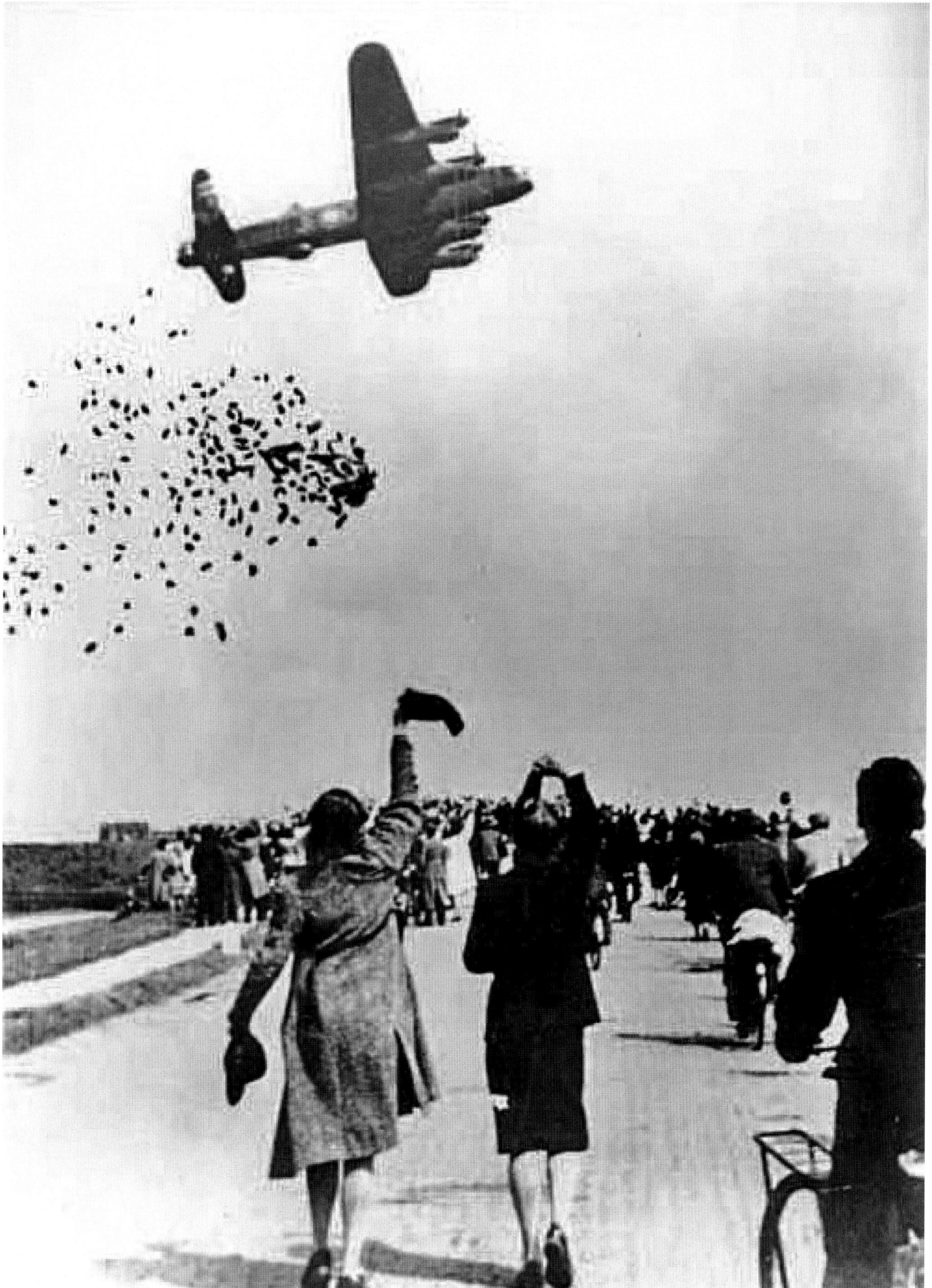

Chapter V – THE END OF THE WAR

The war was officially over May 5th, 1945. I remember that the Germans left in trucks and wagons in a real hurry to get back to Germany. A few days later the first Allied soldiers to show up in our village were Canadians. They set up a distribution camp in the village square and began to hand out food to the villagers. Initially, this consisted of big five-gallon tins of strange round thick crackers. We were told not to eat too many of these or we would swell up and die. And the bread they were handing out was something we had never seen before. It was pure white, unlike any bread we baked. Our bread was always brown because we did not have or use bleached flour to make white bread.

Above: German soldiers and equipment retreating to Germany at the end of the war. In the foreground, Mister Dutchman's facial expression is priceless....a subtle good riddance!!!

Holland has set May 4th of each year as a national day of mourning and flowers are laid out all over the countryside. There are many monuments throughout Holland commemorating those who sacrificed themselves for others and of their bravery and battles fought. In Amsterdam, the Anne Frank house is now a museum and receives a million visitors annually.

Anne Frank was born in Germany in 1929 and moved to Holland with her family in 1938 following Hitler's rise to power. Anne's father, Otto Frank, was in the banking business in Germany but that was not an option for him after their move to Holland. Subsequently, Otto Frank set up a small factory next to their residence in Amsterdam where he marketed spices, herbs and pectin's.

When in 1942 the Germans started to round up Jewish people, Anne Frank, her sister, mother and father went into hiding in the attic of the house next to Otto Frank's small factory. Four employees of Otto's business joined them. Someone eventually tipped off the German Secret Police and the little group's hiding place was raided in 1944. The Frank family and Otto's employees were subsequently captured, split up and sent to various concentration camps, including the notorious Auschwitz. German concentration camps were essentially 'death camps' and the only person to survive was Otto Frank. Otto was in Auschwitz when it was liberated by the Soviet army in January of 1945.

Upon his return to Amsterdam Otto Frank recovered 300 loose papers his daughter Anne had written as a diary while in hiding. Otto Frank knew his daughter always wanted to become an author and from those pages, with help from the Dutch government, he produced a manuscript that later became a book. Mr. Frank dedicated his life to the memory of his daughter and his book, *THE DIARY OF ANNE FRANK,* sold over tens of millions of copies worldwide. The book was also made into a movie that was equally as popular. The Anne Frank museum allows people to climb the narrow stairway of the house and walk through the door behind a bookcase where they stand in awe of the small attic room rooms the Frank family hid for more than two years.

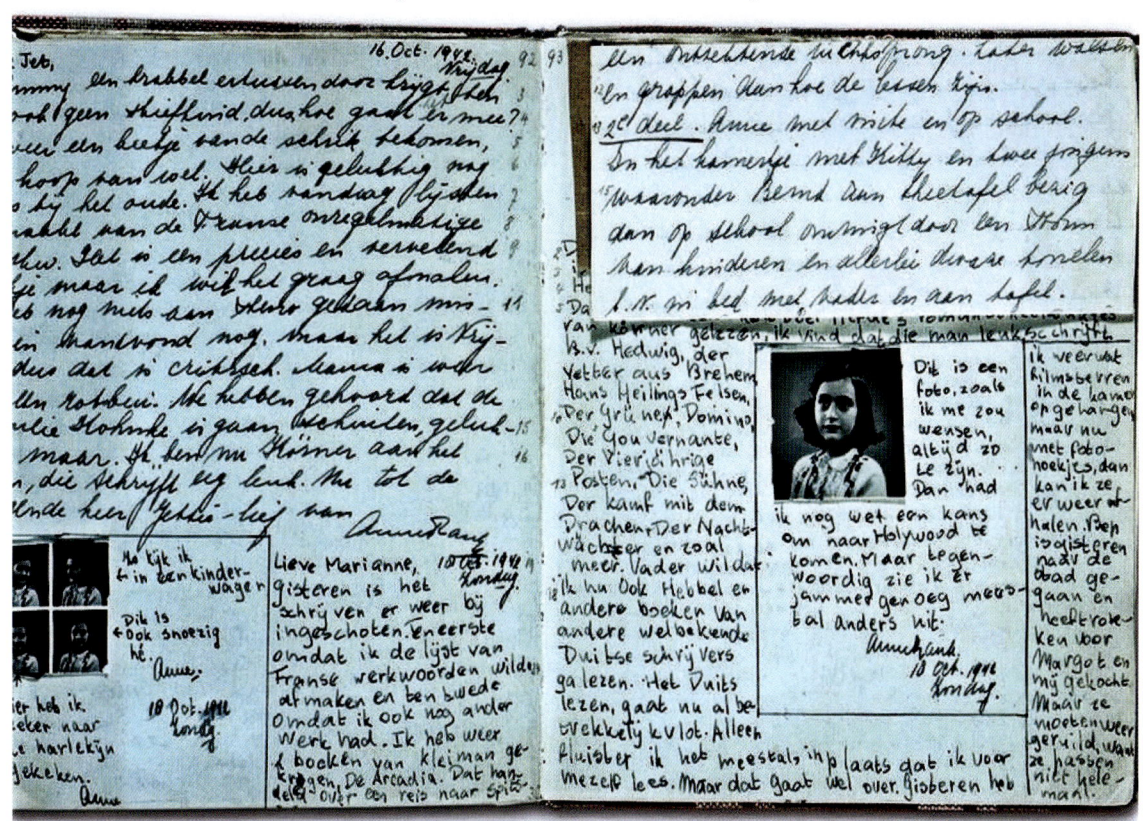

Excerpt: Anne Frank diary

Shortly after the war we were allowed back to survey our flooded homes, if they were accessible. I can still recall taking our bikes over the dykes to our home. Fortunately, we had placed our belongings upstairs and they had fared well. However, many other houses were broken into by looters, pilfered and suffered a lot of damage.

Our house upon our return at the end of the war.

The government installed huge auger like pumps to remove the saltwater from the flooded polders. The process was very slow and it took months to remove water to a point where the land started to show again.

Auger Pumps

It was a real sight. There wasn't a single living thing as result of the land being covered in salt water for over a year. It took a couple of years for the land to be productive again. Since our house fared so well, and was livable, we were among the first people allowed back into the recovered land. It was months earlier than the people in the village whose property was located in deeper water.

Being back home earlier than most people we went out to explore the countryside and the big dunes overlooking the North Sea where Germans built structures we were never allowed close enough to see. We wanted to see what the Germans had left behind and if there was anything useful. And maybe discover souvenirs of war.

There were huge storage yards close to grandma Snoek's house where the Germans had stored all sorts of things. It was mostly big equipment we couldn't use for anything but there were a lot of smaller items the villagers were picking up and taking home. Rifles and pistols were the favorites, as well as ammunition and hand grenades -- those with wooden handles. Before the government put a fence around the compounds dad liked to pick up flare gun shells, but he never found a pistol. What dad did to fire the shells was to bore a small hole near the base of the shell, pour out a little powder, then stand the shell upright and light the powder. The shell would go off, shooting a fireball high in the air that looked just like fireworks. One time when dad was lighting off a shell it fell over after he lit it. Wow, what a recoil! The shell came shooting back, hit my dad's hand and made a nice round burn mark on the back of his hand.

German Stockpiles

For a short period after the war we kids were still able to get into that ammo dump and managed to collect a few German souvenirs. Most prized was the wooden handled grenade we purloined and planned to use at a later date. Our grenade was well hidden because we surely didn't want our parents to know we even had anything like that.

German hand grenade.

As life slowly got back to normal after the war we were anxious to try out our hand grenade for fishing. We had seen adults use them and how easily they caught fish. It was now time for us to find out for ourselves how many fish we could catch. Not wanting to get caught we had to try one out at a canal a long way from home and away from anyone who could see us.

When we found such a canal we unscrewed the safety cap on the end of the grenades wooden handle, pulled the pin and pitched it into the water. Oh boy! Being the grenade was under water when it went off some of the noise was muffled but it still was a good-sized explosion. It was amazing! The blast either killed the fish or the concussion knocked them out and they just floated to the surface. All we had to do then was gather up the fish with a net on a long pole. It didn't take us long to fill up a sack of fish we could take home.

Knowing we would get questioned as to how we were able to catch so many fish we divided them up so each of us had a nice batch to take home. Mom was sure surprised with all the fish and we told her we had set out nets to catch that many. Nets were generally used for catching eel and fish caught by using a fishing pole but mom must have believed our story. Whew! She didn't question us again and when dad got home that night we had a great fish dinner.

As the water started to recede little islands would appear and because the water wasn't very deep dad would take Cor and me out to them. Ducks and gulls nested all over those little islands and we would go around gathering eggs. Since the eggs were fresh mom would cook them for us to eat.

For a couple of years following land reclamation there wasn't much vegetation growth. The soil remained too salty, which meant the potato business was very slow. Dad had to find other work until the Van Hennik company was back in production. We managed okay, however, because there was a lot of work available and a huge shortage of workers.

Shortly after the war ended in 1945 grandpa and grandma Vander Waal celebrated their 50th wedding anniversary. Most of the area around Oudenhoorn was still underwater due to the dykes Germans had breached to flood the lowlands. But that did not deter the family as most of grandpa and grandma's sixteen children, and about twenty grandchildren, were present to celebrate. Dad's sister Trien and her daughter, who was Corrie's and my age, were also there to take part in the festivities.

All the family with grandpa and grandma Vander Waal
Corrie, Cor and me being held up on shoulders

Grandpa and grandma with grandchildren
Corrie, Cor and me in front row

My youngest brother, Hugo, was born March 10th, 1946. Mom told Cor and me to ride our bikes to grandma Snoek's to visit for the day. Hugo was born about the middle of the day with the assistance of a midwife.

Memories of grandpa Jacob Vander Waal are very vague. We didn't visit them very often because they lived near the big sea dyke that, during the war, had been off limits to many people. We just did not seem to have as much fun there as we did at grandpa Snoek's.

Grandma Vander Waal passed away in 1946 and shortly thereafter grandpa Vander Waal was moved to a nursing home in the village. That didn't last long, however, as he got very sick and was moved to aunt Aaght's who lived in town next to our school. Dad took Cor and me to aunt Aaght's house to see grandpa Vander Waal. He told us grandpa was very sick and not expected to live much longer. I can remember seeing grandpa lying in bed and, because he didn't move, not certain he was even alive. Grandpa Vander Waal passed away a couple of days later at the age of 82. It was about the time we migrated to America.

Chapter VI – REBUILDING AND VISITS

In our village of Oudenhoorn dad's sister, aunt Aaght, was in the milk distribution business on a very small scale. Her two girls, Zoetje and Neeltje, teenagers about ten years older than me, would go from door to door distributing milk. The girls had a special box on their bicycles to carry the milk. They later acquired a small pony cart that carried a lot more milk and thus able to expanded their deliveries. Aunt Aaght's house was right next to my school. Before I went home from school I would stop there often to visit the girls and enjoy one of my aunt's snacks.

Zoetje and Neeltje

It had been some time since we were allowed to travel freely throughout the country and when restrictions were lifted we wasted no time getting around to see and visit many of our relatives. We were now free to take the train to the city for a visit with dad's sister, Trien Vander Werf, and cousin Corrie who was my age. They lived in the city of Den Haag where dad's other sister, Rena, lived and owned a small restaurant/deli. Aunt Trien and her husband Tuin worked for Rena by running the small restaurant located close to the city's 'red light district'. *(NOTE: Prostitution was, and still is, legal in Holland.)* When not 'working' a bunch of the 'gals' would be in the restaurant having coffee and a sandwich. They seemed to be a close-knit group of girls who looked out for each other.

When in Den Haag all of us would end up on the beach not far from there. The beach went for miles and a place we could swim in the North Sea. Today that area is part of Scheveningen, a massive resort open year round and draws people from all over Europe. Scheveningen includes all sorts of carnival type entertainment, as well as hundreds of restaurants and fast food places.

Scheveningen – then

Scheveningen – now

Another memory about going to Den Haag is of all the stores we didn't have in the village where we lived. One of our favorite stores was the licorice store where they had a huge variety of licorice --- some sweet, some salty and hundreds of different shapes and sizes. Licorice is extremely popular in Holland and was about the only thing sold in that 'winkel' (store).

Just outside of Den Haag the government had set up hundreds of land plots for city dwellers to garden. Uncle Teun spent weekends working one of those plots and visiting with other gardeners who also shared a common interest -- to provide food for their families. It was a strange sight seeing all those small gardens with little tool sheds for gardeners to stay in when it rained and keep their garden tools out of the weather. Their plots seemed really small to us. Our gardens in the countryside were huge and we grew things like potatoes and beans that took up a lot of room. Plus, we always raised a pig that ate all the waste food and vegetables. We would get a pig in the spring and by fall it was large enough for slaughter. A butcher would come out, kill the pig, cover it with straw, and then light it on fire, which burned all the hair off the pig so it was really smooth. Everything on the pig was eaten. Nothing was wasted. Blood was drained to make blood sausage and the intestines used for sausages liners. The entire head was cooked and the meat taken out to grind up for headcheese. We kids always got the pigs tail --- a treat to eat.

Aunt Trien's family would often take the train to our place in Oudenhoorn and spend a weekend with us. They had been doing this since they got married and, with most of the VanderWaal family living around Oudenhoorn, it was a real treat for everyone. Corrie later told me she always looked forward to coming out for a visit because she got to sleep between us boys at night.

We kids would ride our bikes past grandma Snoek's place on the way to Hellevoetsluis, an old Navy town that had the only movie theater in our area. It was a good ten-mile trip on the bike but we would go for the afternoon matinee. We usually went to see American movies about cowboys because we knew that one day we would get approval to travel to America. We wanted to know all about America but, BOY, were we later in for a surprise --- cowboy movies did not accurately portray America.

One of the last movies we saw before coming to America was 'The Four Feathers'. It is a movie taken from the classic novel written in 1902 by the British writer A E W Mason. The movie takes place in Africa on the Eastern Sudan next to Egypt. There are huge battle scenes between Muslims, local natives and British Foreign Legion. It is a great movie with a lot of action. Over the years six movies based on the classic book were made. The one we saw was the 1939 version in color and shot in many of the actual African locations. It got rave reviews and rated as the best one ever made. The latest version was filmed in 2002.

The Four Feathers movie review posters

The movie is of a period during which the Dutch and British were settling in Africa, a time that parallels what was happening in America when settlers were fighting Indians in the west. They even used similar covered wagons in the movie. As opposed to the British in the north, most Dutch settlers ended up near the southern tip of Africa, known as the Cape Town area. There were many fights between local Zulus and the Dutch during the Boer War. Years later we saw The Four Feathers again on TV. It was still a great movie.

The Four Feathers – Battle Scene

In addition to going to movies in the summer time we would stop at grandma Snoek's to go swimming in the canal in front of her house. The canal had to be at least 300 ft wide and when we got good enough we would swim across to the other side and back.

Grandma Snoek's house on the canal

Swimming in the canal

Grandma Snoek lived about five miles from Helevoetsluis, a city with a long history connected to the sea. Helevoetsluis grew from a little town in the beginning of the 17th century to become the homeport for the Dutch war fleet. The port could accommodate the entire fleet within a land-enclosed fortress having dockside facilities and shops.
NOTE: Old Helevoetsluis map and recent aerial photo contained in Chapter II.

In later years the city was intensely fortified and became a unique combination of fortified city and naval port. A number of famous Dutch admirals, including Piet Heyn, had their home base there. In 1688, during the glorious Revolution, the William III of Orange invasion fleet departed from this port. Today the entire fortress and fortifications are available to the public.

The port of Hellevoetsluis was used During World War II as a base for a number of German naval operations. One in particular was to site the **BIBER**, Germany's secret mini submarine that was to be used to attack coastal shipping. The Biber was a mere 29' long with a beam of 5' 3" and designed to be operated by one man. It could carry two externally mounted torpedoes but had top speeds of only 6.5 knots on the surface and 5.3 submerged.

The Biber mini submarines

Construction of the Biber did not start until early 1944 and the first became operational in August 1944. Over three hundred were built in the twelve-month period before the end of the war. Officially, Bibers were called the K-Flotille 261. In addition to seaports near us, from where they operated, Hellevoetsluis and Rotterdam, Bibers were also deployed from Belgium, Denmark and Norway.

The Biber had a severe failure rate as result of its many limitations. They were difficult to operate and experienced serious buoyancy problems due to small compensation tanks that made them almost impossible to maintain periscope depth. Inadequate fuel supply equated to an extremely short range of about 100 miles and, as result, they had to be towed by tugboats to their area of operation.

Records show that on December 23rd and 24th, 1944, a fleet of eighteen Biber submarines was dispatched from Hellevoetsluis and Rotterdam. As the flotilla was, being towed out to sea a surprise attack by the British inflicted major casualties. Four Bibers were immediately sunk, one mined and another so severely damaged it was no longer functional. The remaining twelve simply disappeared. Their operational 'success' was one small freighter. Again, in late December eleven more Bibers were deployed but none returned.

Thirty-one Bibers had been lost by the end of 1944 and those remaining were fifteen in Hellevoetsluis and twenty in Rotterdam. All Biber operations ceased on the 28th of April 1945. There had been 142 Biber sorties that resulted in sinking of only 18,450 tons of shipping and damage to two ships. A large number of Bibers were sunk by the British and it is estimated at least thirty-five had been lost due to bad weather. During and following the war many Biber submarines washed up on the beaches of Holland.

Biber washed up on beach

Today there are Biber mini submarines on display in museums in Holland and England.

Biber Mini Submarine with torpedoes attached

Helevoetsluis also had a fishing fleet that would fish the North Sea. Because it was a naval and fishing port, it had its share of taverns and dance halls and became the social place of the region. This is where my mother grew up as a young girl. It was an exiting place to visit and watch all the boats and ship traffic.

On the other corner of the island stood the fortified town of Den Briel. It was on the opposite corner of the island from the small village of Rokanje where our Uncle Bram had his fruit growing business. Rokanje also faces a large waterway and has been a historic seaport dating back to 1306. For centuries the fortress, with its many bastions that protruded from its main walls, completely surrounded and protected the village inside. It is a well-preserved fortress with gun emplacements, city gates and towers. Over the years the town has vastly expanded outside the fortress walls.

Den Briel has its own harbor and commercial fleet that trades with countries all around the Baltic Sea. During the 'Eighty Year War' with Spain there were many fierce assaults against the fortress. Den Briel is about half the size as Hellevoetsluis but both were very important seaports during the 16th and 17th centuries.

Den Briel was a long trip on bicycles but, as we got older, we would occasionally ride there.

Den Briel Fort
1869 Map

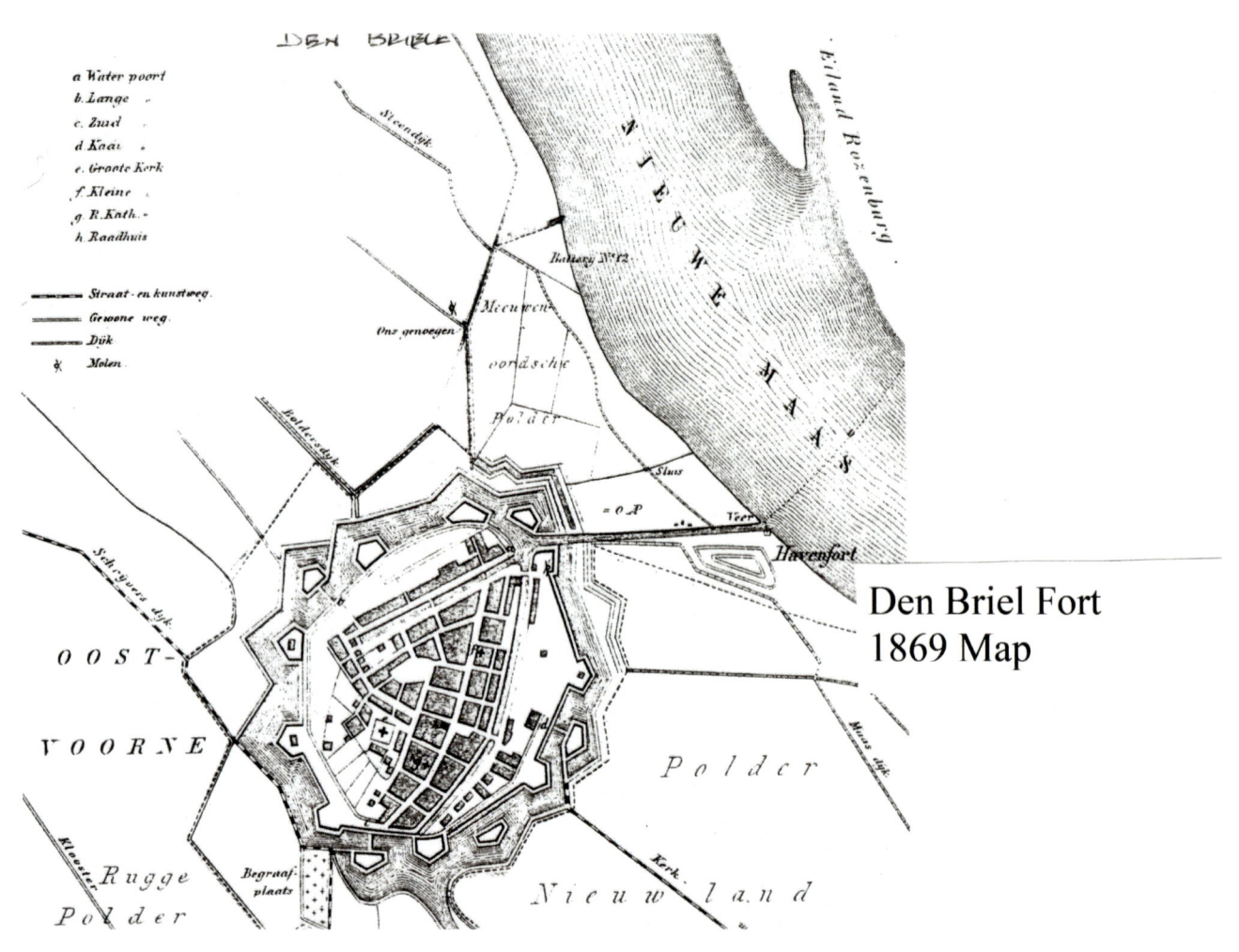

Den Briel Today – Old Fortress Ramparts And Moat Still Exist

There were only two girls in the Snoek family, mom and her sister Marie. Marie was twelve years younger than my mother so mom was grandma's helper. There were seven boys. Born in 1911, mom was the third oldest child. Mom did most of the cooking and cleaning in the house. She also looked after her younger brother, Wim, the last of their children and born with "downs syndrome".

Wim, with
Grandpa and Grandma Snoek

Wim was basically raised by my mother. He was a very unusual child who couldn't talk but had a gibberish language of his own. He was unusually clean and would sometimes change his clothing several times a day. His shirts always had to be perfectly clean and were generally white. He never mastered riding a bicycle so he walked everywhere. He was extremely friendly and everyone in town knew him. Wim would always help people, especially with cleaning. He lived on little tips people gave him which also made him happy and proud. Wim lived an unusually long time for someone with his condition and passed away at sixty years old. At the time he was living with one of the older boys on the Island of Texel.

A few miles from grandma Snoek's house was a bridge that I remember to this day. It was called the Flotbrug. Translated, it would be called a floating bridge. It spanned the Voornse Canal and was of a design used all over Holland prior to today's structural or drawbridge type. They were a pontoon bridge that would float on the water with sections that telescoped out of the way for ships to pass. Most were replaced later for drawbridges that took less maintenance.

How a Flotbrug (Float Bridge) works

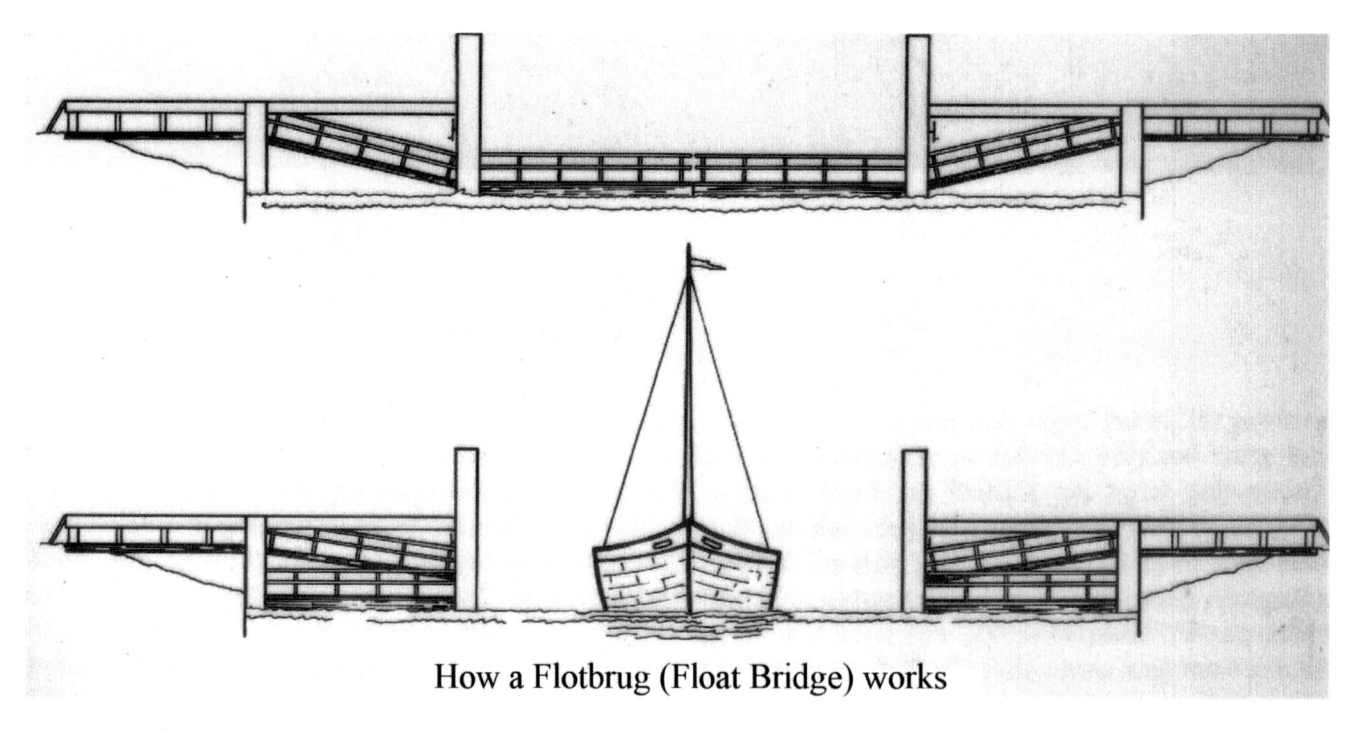

A typical Flotbrug

Chapter VII – DUTCH CUSTOMS AND FOODS

I remember the Christmas holiday in Holland being celebrated differently than in America. First came Saint Nickolas Eve on December 5th followed by Saint Nickolas Day on the 6th. Saint Nickolas, known as 'Saint Nick', traveled throughout the land on a white horse and with him was a black Moorish helper named 'Pete' who handled the horse and carried a bag of 'goodies' for the children. As they traveled Pete would throw the children 'pepernote', a hard baked cookie about the size of a marshmallow. Pepernote is a traditional treat in Holland.

Saint Nickolas and Pete

It is said Saint Nickolas and Pete would travel from Spain but never established how he managed to get around all of Europe in one night. Maybe it is similar to how Santa Claus does in his sleigh pulled by reindeer. The legend of Saint Nickolas dates back to 271 AD and based on a true figure known for his good deeds, helping the poor, and spreading goodwill throughout Europe.

Saint Nickolas Day Celebration

Just before children went to bed on Saint Nickolas Eve they would put their wooden shoes near the stove or fireplace and stuff them with hay and carrots for Saint Nick's horse. The next morning the hay would be gone and small gifts placed near their wooden shoes.

Saint Nickolas and Pete delivering gifts

Festivities would start on Saint Nickolas Eve and continue on Saint Nickolas Day when gifts were exchanged and we were served pastry dolls and 'botterletters' (butterletter), a flaky pastry stuffed with almond paste.

Botterletters are very popular Dutch pastries are usually served during the holiday period. A number of various recipes for botterletters are available on the internet but the real trick is getting the flaky outside crust. A great way to get this done and save a lot of time is to use *Pepperidge Farm* frozen sheets of dough. Simply thaw the dough, roll it a little thinner then add the almond paste mix. They will come out just as good as the original Dutch botterletters and taste great.

Botterletters

December 25th and 26th are national holidays and families would again exchange gifts. These two days are founded upon religious beliefs and not as festive as Saint Nickolas Day. However, these were days we put up our Christmas tree and decorated it with ornaments and strings of silver foil. When I was a child there were no electric lights for the tree. Instead, we had small candles placed in candleholders clamped to tree branches. We had to carefully place the candles to make sure they would not catch the tree on fire. There was always a bucket of water near the tree because if a fire started it had to be quickly put out or the whole tree would catch fire. In all, tree lighting was a special time.

New Years Eve was always a big event for our family and a time for sharing oliebollen, a dough ball using a lot of yeast to make it rise and light then usually blended with some fruit or raisins. The dough would be scooped from a bowl then dropped into hot oil where it would expand into a ball. When it came out of the hot oil it was covered with powdered sugar. Oliebollen always made New Years Eve special when served with fruit, other goodies and special drinks,. On New Years Day we kids would go through the neighborhood wishing people 'Gelukkig Niewjaar' (Happy New Year) and, in turn, given a few coins for good luck in the coming year.

Oliebollen

Another big holiday was a 'Dutch Birthday' that, in large families, seemed to be ongoing. It is distinctively a Dutch celebration. People close to the birthday person would drop by to wish them 'Hartelyk Gefeliciteerd" (Happy Birthday) and be served all sorts of pastries and cookies, as well as cheese and crackers. We kids really enjoyed birthdays because it was a time for us to visit relatives.

At birthday celebrations it was common for all the men to congregate in one part of the house to discuss work and business and smoke cigars or pipes. They would also have the favorite national drink, 'borrel', which is usually Old or New Jenever but better known as 'Dutch Gin' --- a very different gin drink with a juniper flavoring. It wasn't anything we kids were interested in because it was very strong and didn't taste very good.

Advocaat and Boerenjongen

Ladies would retire elsewhere, usually in the kitchen, and have their special drinks, which was either Advocaat or Boerenjongen. Those were drinks we kids did like. Advocaat is a yellow creamy drink made from egg yolk and brandy and very easy to drink. Boerenjongens (farm boys) is sort of nickname for a drink traditionally served at Christmas or weddings but people, especially ladies, like to drink it any time. It is made by soaking raisins in a pan then cooking them just long enough to be softened. Spices and brandy are then added and the mixture put on glass containers and sealed for at least three months before being served in small glasses.

The Dutch remind themselves of birthdays by hanging a birthday calendar in conspicuous place, usually near or in the bathroom. The calendar has loose pages for each month of the year where are written dates of births, deaths and wedding anniversaries for everyone in the family.

Some of the foods we ate as kids stand out in my memory because they were (and are) different than food we eat here in America. A Dutch breakfast was often a 'botterham' which is Dutch for sandwich and consisted of a couple of slices of bread filled with either jam, sliced meats, good Dutch cheese or some other ingredient. Botterhams are made in all sorts of flavors and probably the most popular thing to eat in Holland. For kids it usually included chocolate sprinkles that would stick to the butter. There were also 'pannekoeken' which is Dutch for pancakes, but not like those we eat here. Pannekoeken are very thin, almost like a crepe, and served rolled up and covered with butter, sugar or fruit.

Pannekoeken

Another breakfast we had was 'uitsmyter', interpreted as 'throw-out', and consisted of a slice of buttered bread covered with sliced beef or ham, cheese on top of that, a fried egg placed over the cheese then covered by another slice of buttered bread. These were basically a botterham that could be eaten anytime but usually served at the end of an evening event or party. They are now served almost everywhere as a quick meal 'on the go'.

Croquettes are a very popular sort of finger food often served in fast food restaurants and self-service food bars but can also be bought in grocery stores. They are made with a soft filling that can be a roux (mixture) of beef, chicken, or possibly seafood, and usually served hot. The roux is precooked, allowed to cool, then formed into an elongated ball. It is then dipped into a mixture of milk, flour and breadcrumbs then deep-fried. Viola!

A treat that has a crispy outside with a soft tasty filling. Croquettes can be eaten with a salad as a meal or also as an 'on the go' food. A smaller and just as tasty version of the croquette is a 'bitter ballen'. This little goody is usually served as an appetizer and often found to be a 'bar snack' in pubs,

Croquettes and Bitter Ballen

The potato is a major staple in Holland and one of its uses is a favorite street food called Patat or Friets. I believe the concept originally came from France, hence they are called French fries here. They are sold everywhere, usually in a paper cone, with a big dollop of mayonnaise or something similar on top for dipping the fries. Friets were never served with ketchup although a lot of tourists are now asking for it and some places provide it as a option.

At right is a typical street friet.

Several years after we left for the United States a massive potato processing plant was built in the village of Oudenhoorn. This was probably due to the village being located in one of the largest potato growing areas in Holland. The plant is mostly automated but employs several hundred employees. Most interesting is seeing raw potatoes going in one end of the plant and frozen 'friets' coming out the other. The facility is located near the big sea dyke, about five miles from our house and on the same road, 'the Molendyke'.

The 'poffertje' is also a street vendor food and looks like a tiny fluffy pancake. It is cooked on a special stovetop that has small indentations. Poffertjes usually come in an order of a dozen, covered with butter and powered sugar. These, too, are a mouthwatering dish and dimpled pans can be purchased for making poffertjes at home.

Poffertjes

Poffertje Vendor

'Stroopwaffles' are a Dutch delight that is among the top ten foods one must try while in Holland. These are made on round waffle irons that have a distinct pattern and about 6 inches in diameter. Stroopwaffle dough is very thin and two waffles are made into a small sandwich with a caramel filling then baked to completion. Stroopwaffles are usually eaten like a cookie but most people like to warm them before eating by placing it on top of their hot cup of tea or coffee. Some stroopwaffle packaging depicts this method of warming.

At right: Stroopwaffles

The original stroopwaffles were made in 1840 in the city of Gouda. Stroopwaffles grew in popularity and by the 1960's, in Gouda alone, there were 17 factories producing stroopwaffles. This wonderful treat is sold by street vendors, at mini marts and at supermarkets throughout Holland. And the demand just keeps growing. Their popularity has expanded worldwide, and to the extent they can be purchased on Amazon. McDonalds even offers a stroopwaffle McFlurry.

'Snert' is a Dutch soup and great wintertime meal. It is an old Dutch recipe for pea soup that is quite thick and nothing like our American version. The basic soup is still split pea with a nice piece of ham bone or pork chops added after the peas are well cooked. But unlike pea soup here, many other ingredients, such as potatoes, carrots, leeks, celery and diced sausage, are added. That mixture is then cooked at length to absorb the great flavors of all the ingredients. During cold winters snert is a good wholesome meal, usually accompanied with Dutch cheese and bread, It is so tasty and very filling.

Snert

One dinner course I remember my mother making was from a recipe dating back to the 'Eighty Year War' with Spain during the 1600's. It was called 'hutspot', a carrot and potato stew with a few onions and short ribs or sausage tossed in for flavor.

At left: Hutspot

A dish similar to hutspot is called 'stampot'. It has no real English meaning other than what was being cooked being mashed or 'stamped'. The recipe called for a lot of carrots that when mashed made the dish come out a bright orange carrot color. Then there was a dish called 'boerekool', or farmers cabbage in Dutch, and used fresh kale instead of carrots and onions. It was usually served with sausage. A very popular side dish was Dutch Red Cabbage, or 'Hollandse Rode Kool', and comprised of red cabbage, onions, apples, and vinegar added for flavor.

Stampot

The Dutch are very well known for eating fish and, in particular, herring. When in season, which starts in late spring, they are usually served from herring stands or carts. Herring can be served whole, fresh raw or raw salted. They also come pickled with onions and generally eaten 'as is' or with bread. Eel, or 'paling' in Dutch, once was a really cheap fish but are now in limited supply and very expensive. Paling can be bought alive to be fried but the most popular way today is smoked.

Paling   Paling sandwich

Because eel are considered fish we would use long fishing poles to catch them in the canals. But, the better way was by using a hoop net, which consisted of a series of hoops connected by a net in between that got smaller as it went to the end. We would set the nets overnight and eel would swim in and get trapped. There were lots of eel in the canals around us.

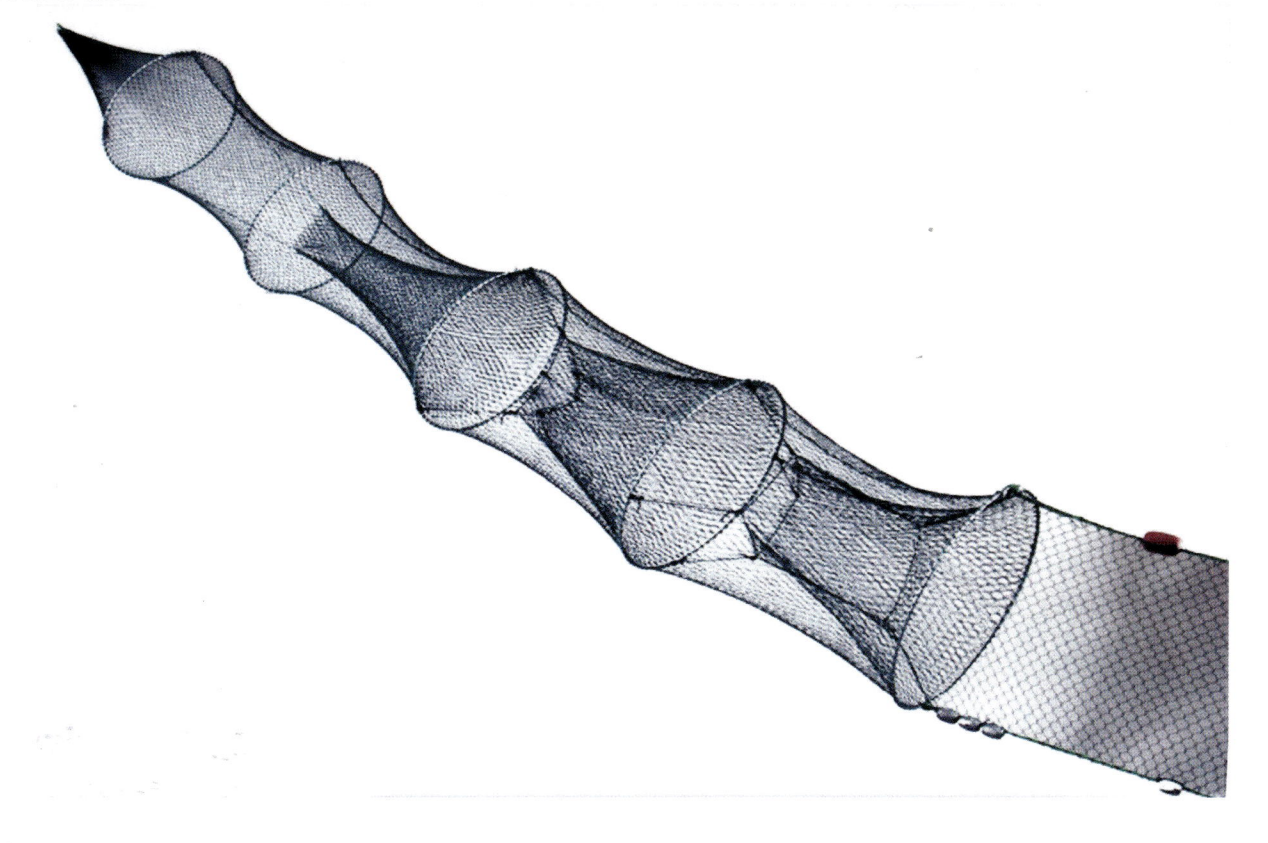

A typical paling net

A more popular fish to eat are sole, or in Dutch called 'Tong'. They are generally served deep-fried. The small sole are called 'tongetjes'.

A couple of other dishes worth writing about are a Dutch dinner salad and, believe it or not, horse meat.

The Dutch dinner salad is sort of a cross between a green salad and a potato salad. We only ate the salad during the summer months when our own garden would produce fresh red lettuce. The dish can be a complete meal in of itself and something we still eat today is red lettuce is available in stores year round.

The recipe consists of frying several strips of bacon then removing them from the pan for later use in the salad. To the grease in the pan add about ¼ cup of red wine vinegar, 3 teaspoons of water, 2 ½ teaspoons of sugar and salt and pepper to taste. Bring the mixture to a boil then set aside for use as the dressing. Pick 6 cups of leaves from stems of red lettuce, add diced green onions. Cook several small yellow potatoes (for each person to be served) until soft. Remember the Dutch eat potatoes with almost every meal. Break the bacon slices into bits.

Build the salad by placing hot potatoes on each persons plate, smash them with a fork, add a dollop of butter, cover the potatoes with mixture of greens then sprinkle with bacon bits.

Spoon heated dressing over the salad then garnish with hot sliced hardboiled eggs. Enjoy!

The other dish – horse meat – is one we have not had since leaving Holland as it is difficult to obtain here in America. When I was growing up in Holland horses were used extensively. Every farm had a team or two for pulling wagons full of produce or hay from the fields. And, because gasoline was in short supply during the war, horses were used in many capacities by the German army. Generally, these would be the huge Belgium workhorses.

When an injured horse could not be mended it would be euthanized and its meat sold to a butcher shop in the village. When 'word' got out that a butcher had horse meat for sale the local people lined to buy what they considered a real treat – and sold out in a day.

Mom would cook a horse meat roast in her 'Dutch Oven' on top of the stove. In fact, everything we cooked was on top of the stove because there were no ovens. Coal was used to fuel the stove as it made a very hot fire and lasted longer than wood. Horse meat is extremely lean, with almost no fat at all, and made a great tasting roast. Plus, the leftover roast could be eaten on bread for days.

Note: Most recipes for Dutch dishes mentioned in this book are available on the internet (Google).

Chapter VIII – SCHOOL AND SPORTS

Except for the year our area was flooded by the Germans, necessitating our move to Abbenbroek, I attended school from kindergarten through sixth grade in Oudenhoorn. Our return to Oudenhoorn was about the time I started sixth grade.

My school in Oudenhoorn

School classes started at 8:30 in the morning. A half hour lunch break was had at noon and we went home at 4:00 in the afternoon. Students attended class full days Monday through Friday and a half-day on Saturday. It was a method of education applied in Holland that allowed completion of school after the sixth grade, which would be the equivalent of an eighth grade level here in the States.

At right: A very studious fellow, me 1942

Our school had a large gymnasium that was used for all sorts of functions. Athletics were part of our daily schooling and we learned all sorts of sports, from rope climbing to foot racing. And, we suffered those dull exercise routines. If weather was good we went outside, if not the gym was used for all those activities.

A predominate schoolyard pastime for boys was marble games. In Dutch they were called 'knikkeren'. Every kid had a favorite glass marble called a 'knikker' that he played as his own special marble. There were a number of different marble games, one to suit every taste. We kept our marbles in a little bag that was usually made by your mother and it was your prized possession. Girls usually kept busy during lunchtime and recess playing a mixed bag of skip rope or hopscotch.

Playing knikker   Prized possessions

There was usually bicycle racing after school. That was, a sport better suited for bigger kids who had the power because we Vander Waals, being of smaller stature, never really stood a chance against the big guys. Outside of school, 'kick the can' was always fun and at dusk we often played hide and seek.

Other games we played were various round ball games and, of course, Holland's national game of football. Our football is what we call soccer here in the States.

A sport almost as active as soccer was 'Korfball'. It is somewhat similar to basketball except that, instead of a hoop, an actual basket is used to shoot the ball into. The basket is specially woven, about the same diameter as a basketball hoop, stands about a foot tall, but without a bottom, and mounted on an 11½ ft pole. I think the term basketball might have originated from this game. There was no backboard so all shots were field shots. Each team had eight players so it was a very intense team sport with having to pass the ball to the right player in position to make a field shot. The game could be played indoors or in an open field, which is how I remember playing the game. It is still a very popular sport in Holland.

Korfball (Dutch: *korfbal*) is a ball sport, with similarities to netball and basketball. It is played by two teams of eight players with four female players and four male players in each team. The objective is to throw a ball into a netless basket that is mounted on a 3.5 m (11.5 feet) high pole.

Korfball match at the 1928 Summer Olympics in the Olympic Stadium in Amsterdam

Korfball match in the Netherlands

Korfball

Outdoor korfball match in the Netherlands

Highest governing body	International Korfball Federation
First played	1902
Characteristics	
Contact	Limited
Team members	8 per side: 4 male players and 4 female players
Mixed gender	Yes
Type	Team sport, ball sport
Equipment	Korfball
Venue	Korfball court
Presence	
Olympic	Demonstration sport in 1920 and 1928
World Games	1985–present

Korfball

Some memories of my early school days in Holland really stand out. I remember our school desks had a bench type seat with desk in front for two students and different than those here in the States. One thing we seemed to always be doing was practicing penmanship by properly writing lower and upper case letters in script form. Script examples were posted on little signs all around the classroom. Penmanship was graded all the time and to get a good grade we had to get it right.

VERKLEINDE REPRODUCTIE.

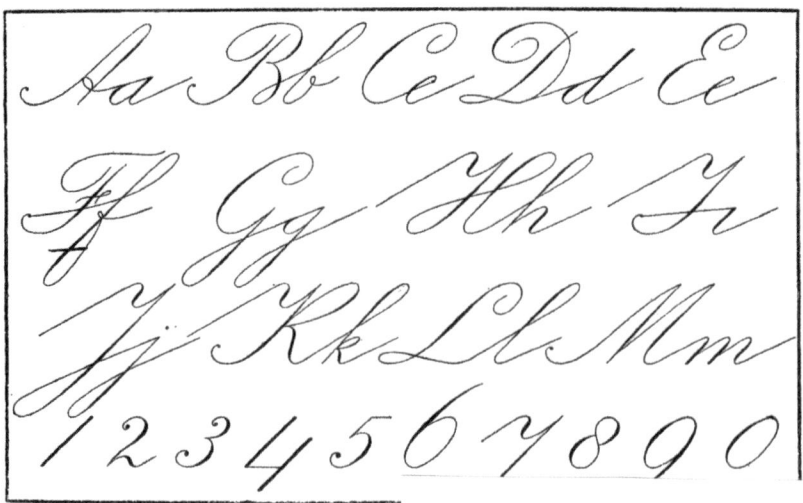

LETTERKAART B.

Hand writing samples that were posted all around our class rooms

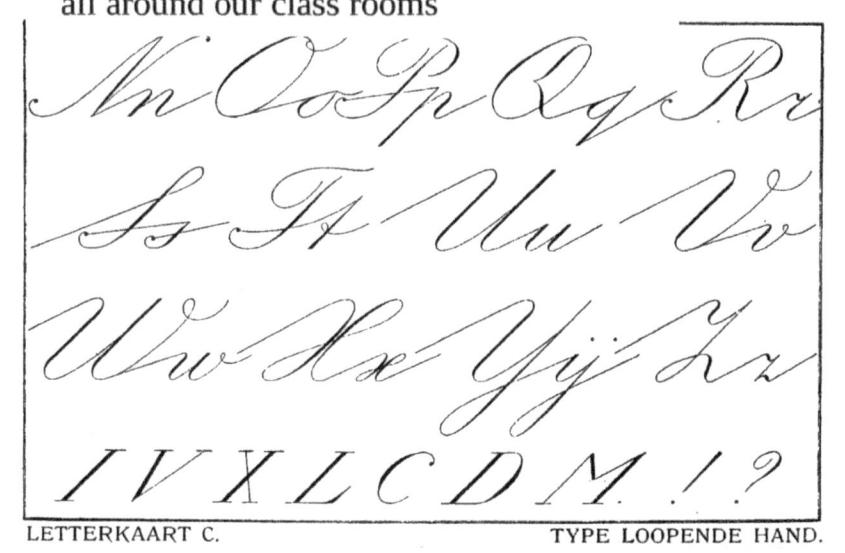

LETTERKAART C.   TYPE LOOPENDE HAND.

In addition to the '3Rs' we had to learn the location and spelling of the Dutch colonies scattered all over the world. We would have to walk up to a big world map, point them out and say the names and location of their large cities. I always had trouble with names of the Dutch East Indies Islands and of the cities on Java, Sumatra and Borneo.

In 1602 the Dutch created a multinational trading empire called the Dutch East India Company and sailed what became the largest trading fleet of ships in the world. The Company traded throughout the world during the 1630 – 1800 period. Because of the European demand for spices --- such as nutmeg, cloves, and cinnamon --- the Dutch East India Company heavily plied Indian Ocean archipelagos. The archipelagos are comprised of over 17,000 islands with only about 900 inhabited. The inhabitants were never unified or ruled by one entity and, to gain control of their resources, Dutch East India traders entered into alliances with local tribe elites and rulers. Over time, many of its employees settled on the islands to live a life of luxury they could never achieve in Holland and, to maintain citizenship in the 'Fatherland', established Dutch colonies. These colonies were initially protected by the Dutch East India Company but later by the Dutch government.

THE DUTCH EAST INDIA COMPANY

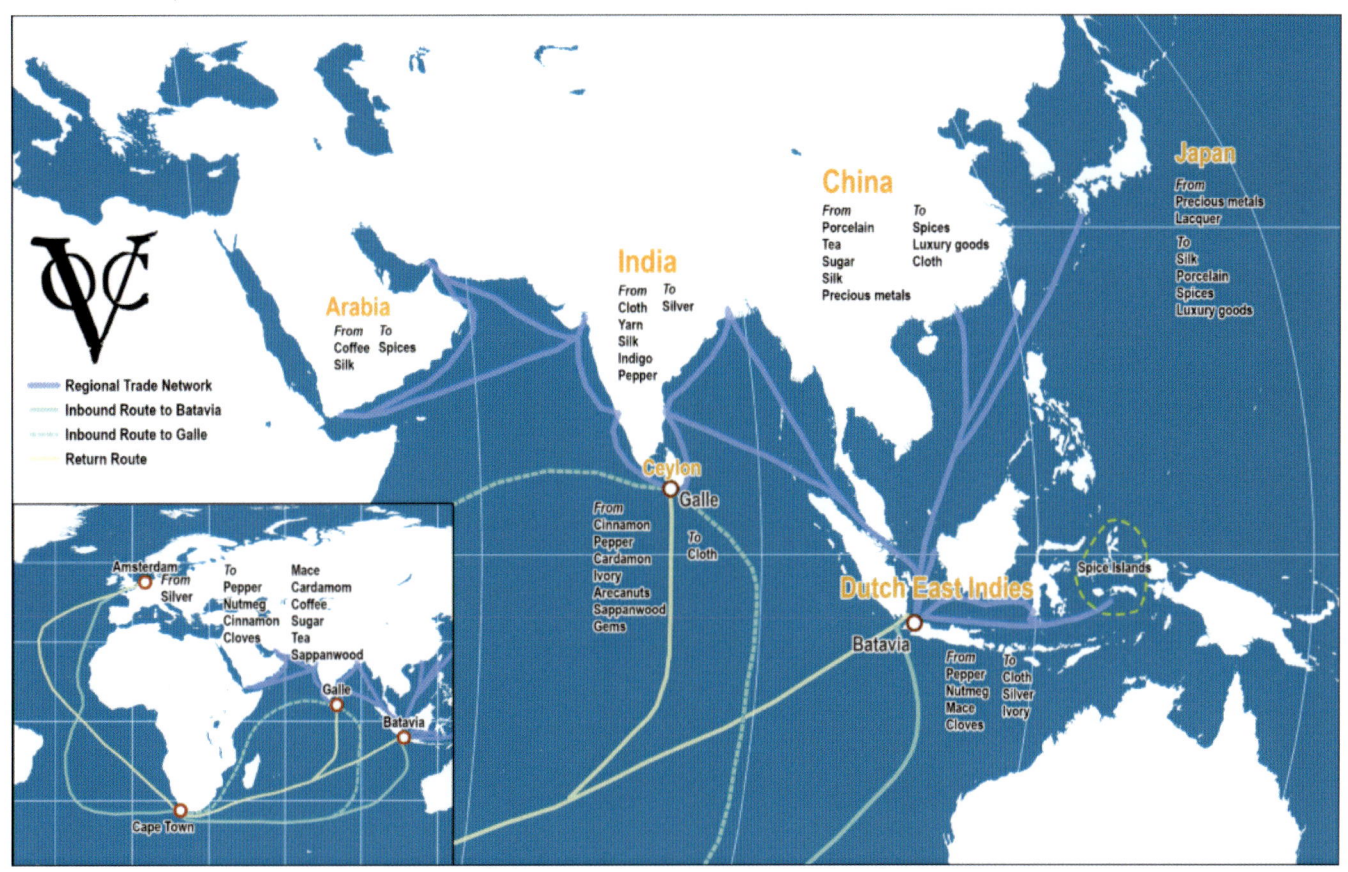

Dutch East India Company trade routes

Types of ships sailed by The Dutch East India Company

In 1624 the Dutch East India Company established a settlement in America on the southern tip of what is now Manhattan Island. The new colony was christened New Amsterdam, later to become known as New York. New Amsterdam grew to encompass the area of present day New York City and parts of Long Island.

Old map of Dutch Colony of Nieuw Amsterdam

Most of New Amsterdam was built by slaves purchased from slave traders who brought them from Africa. At its peak 9000 settlers from various countries, and speaking many languages, were living in the colony. Following a series of battles fought with the British, the settlement was surrendered to England in 1674.

After World War II, on December 27, 1949, the colonized 'Dutch East Indies' was granted independence and became known as the Republic of Indonesia. Indonesian culture, especially the food, has since been brought back to Holland. Today there are many Indonesian Restaurants all over Holland and they are very popular.

Painting of Nieuw Amsterdam

Our schooling was quite regimented and disciplined, particularly in the history of early Dutch explorations throughout the world.

Just getting to school could sometimes be our little Dutch adventures. Dutch winters can be extremely cold and can go on for weeks on end. The winter of 1947 remains in my memory as it was bitter cold that year. The canals, large waterways and lakes had all frozen over, an occurrence of only about every three to four years. However, to our advantage, there were many small canals and drainage ditches on the way to school and wintertime water levels usually very low. Some waterways were down five to six feet below normal, which gave us a bit of shelter from the wind as we walked to school on the ice.

Winter was the only time we boys got to wear long pants. The rest of the year we wore shorts.

Me in my winter garb

I entered sixth grade in the fall of 1947. It would be my last year in school and the end of my required period of education. This was also when I would have to decide where to go to high school, then college, or vocational school. If I opted for higher education it would have meant going to school somewhere else in the country. However, that decision was never made because by then I knew I would be going to school in America.

When I later started school in the United States to be better able to communicate I was enrolled in a basic English language class for a short period of time. I was then put in the third grade where I really felt out of place. Luckily, I was only there for about three months before they moved me up to fifth grade. It was still a year behind where I was in Holland but I did get moved up to sixth grade the next year. Even though I was a year behind it worked out okay since not being a big kid I fit in, just a bit older than my classmates. That did have its advantages, however, because in my sophomore year I was the only kid in class to own a car. This was a huge plus when it came to girls and it seemed I suddenly had a lot more friends.

Being in the Dutch school system allowed me to be way ahead of other students in certain subjects, especially math. My poorest subject was English and I struggle with it to this day.

Chapter IX – COUSIN NEELJTE

I was about eleven years old at the time we were living on the Molendyke. Cor Hoogzant, a relative, had an onion business where farmers brought in onions by wagonload. The Hoogzants had a large building right across the road from us where they would sort, grade and put the onions in sacks. Cor had a crew of about a half dozen guys who worked for him year round.

Cor was married to Zoetje, daughter of my dad's sister Aagt. They had a large house that was full of boarders who were usually all bachelors. Zoetje did all the cooking for them, a major job feeding a bunch of hungry guys. I remember going there occasionally just to see what was going on. Zoetje had huge pots in which she would cook potatoes, vegetables and some type of meat. It always looked like a lot of work to cook that much food.

The guys were very athletic and had all sorts of gym equipment. There were parallel bars, vaulting horses and trapezes. When working out they looked like a bunch of acrobats in a circus act. We kids used to sit and watch them go through their routines, which was generally in the evening after work.

One of those guys was Han Mastenbroek, Zoetje's sister Neeltje's boyfriend. Neeltje was often there to visit Han and help Zoetje. Han was one of the young men who refused to be taken to Germany to work in their war factories and made an escape by boat from Holland to England.

Han wrote an article about his escape and it is included in a book called 'Once Upon a Wartime'. The book was written by Molly Burkett and contains a series of stories about individuals who served during World War II. I have included an excerpt of the book (Han's article) because I feel that what he was and how he became part of the Vander Waal family is so interesting it has to be shared.

At right: Han Mastenbroek

Han was a close friend of Cor Hoogzant as they grew up together on the Island of Goeree Overflakkee, the island next to ours to the south and only accessible by ferry. (See the map of the island at the start of the story.)

Han's dad was a potato merchant and Cors family in the onion business. In 1939, because there was no onion business on our island and a lot of competition among onion farmers on their island, Cor and his two brothers moved to our town. They moved into an old farm on the Molendyk in Oudenhoorn and started their onion business.

When the Germans flooded a large part of our island in 1944, including the village of Oudenhoorn, Cor and Zoetje moved back to his dad's place on the island where he lived before. His dad converted one of his onion sheds to a temporary home for them and where they stayed until the war was over. It was there their son, Kees, was born in Feb 1945.

Cor's two brothers had been picked up and shipped off to Germany to work in the factories. It was about that time the Canadians were liberating the lower islands of Holland and when Han and his buddies made their escape to the liberated part of Holland.

Young Dutchmen rounded up and in detention
before being shipped to Germany

Shortly before his escape Han was able to further his relationship with Neeltje when she came from Oudenhoorn to visit Zoetje and Cor at their temporary home in the onion shed.

Once upon a Wartime VII

by Molly Burkett

BARNY BOOKS

Following is an excerpt from this book --- Escape from Holland by Han Mastenbroek

I was born in 1920 at Sommelsdyk on the Island of Goeree en Overflakkee an Island off the coast of Holland where the rivers Rhine and the Maas empty into the sea. My father was a farmer and when I left school I worked on the farm with my father and my three older brothers. All transport from the Island was by barge and about every village had it's own harbour. We lived in a very close community and my parents were like all our neighbors very strickt and religious. I joined the army in 1940 and couldn't wait to go. This was my chance for some adventure. I had never been off the Island before, and all was great for a few weeks. However, on May 10th the Germans invaded Holland and on May 15th five days later, Holland surrendered.

I had only been in the army for six weeks. We had been out on a training exercise and when we returned to camp the German soldiers where there. They took all our motorized equipment, which had been made in Germany anyway. They then took away all the officers and regular soldiers and kept us recruits in the camp for the next three months, prisoners in our own country. My father and uncle came to see us and asked for our release saying I was needed on the farm, but they wouldn't release me until later in September. When I got home the Germans had already moved onto the Island and the officers horses were stabled on the farm.

I hated the Germans and the more I saw them the more I hated them but my uncle and brothers thought they were great. They actually approved of everything they did. As far as I was concerned, my own uncle and brothers were Nazis. I couldn't even bring myself to talk to them even though we were all working on the same farm. I couldn't trust people in my own family and let alone in the community.

We heard a farmer on the next island hid a British pilot in their barn but some one in the community told the Germans. They took the whole family out and shot them as well as the two men who worked on the farm. There was a strict curfew in place where we were not allowed outside between 8 Pm until 8 Am all people of Jewish faith had to wear a Yellow star on the outside of their clothing. Men and boys would be taken unexpected and taken to labour camps to work in Germany. And all doctors, dentists and teachers were taken away as hostages and all weapons, radios were confiscated. Some people hid their radios but if they were discovered they would end up going to a concentration camp, so we had no idea what was going on in the rest of the world. In 1944 the Germans started to flood the islands by opening up the floodgates in the dykes and people were ordered out of their houses. People had to flee to the main land and find other accommodations..

The atmosphere became tense and people were disappearing and we had no idea what was happening to them. One day when I was visiting my cousin's cafe he drew me aside and warned me that my name was on the wanted list and to be careful. I went immediately underground; I was still living at home but kept out of sight and well away from the Nazi sympathizers like my own uncle and brother.

My friends and I had often discuses what we would do if that situation came up. So now I had a plan that I put into action. I contacted my friend Bram who worked on one of the ferries he said he was ready to come with me to escape from the Island. He said he had four other friends who wanted to come and I also had four guys. We arranged to meet the the next evening and form our plan. However his friends chickened out as well as my friends but we went ahead with a plan without them. The plan depended on getting a small boat down to the southern part of the island. The estuary between Overflakkee and the South mainland was one of the arms of the Rhine delta. We knew the Allies had already occupied the banks on the mainland. We could hear their guns and tanks move about, but the Germans controlled our island and the channel.

Now that most of the island was flooded and refugees and any traffic had to travel over the top of the dykes that were well above the water. This also made it very visual for the Germans to check out what was traveling and then there were all the checkpoints, that were set up at intervals along the roads and you needed a pass to go through them. Then there were the area that were not flooded and those were mined. Most of the troops were stationed at the north end of the Island where the coastal defense was build with bunkers and gun emplacements. There was one large barracks at the southern end of the island and I knew the farmer who carried supplies to the barracks from the ferries. So I went to see him to try to persuade him to carry our boat. However the farmer did not want to be involved, but I bluffed him anyway with some money to make it his worthwhile. He finally agreed to meet us over to the spot where we would have the boat to load on his wagon.

We didn't have the boat yet but I had my eye on a boat that was sitting in the water close to where we could slide it up the bank out of the water. I waited until curfew and went to where the boat was tied up behind one of the houses and undid the rope and rowed it into the harbour, listening every few minutes to make sure no one was watching. I knew none of the local people would be out and it was only the Germans that could be out after curfew. My buddy Bram was waiting for me near the harbor in the shadows ready to help me get the boat out of the water. However the boat was much bigger and heavier than what we anticipated and all the tugging and trying to slide it out of the water didn't work with just the two of us. I went to a friends place for help and see if we could help and store the boat for the night. He said he would help and the three of is managed to get the boat out of the water up the bank and drag it over to my friends barn. We had to be extremely cautious because there were Germans about on patrol and keeping a eye on the harbor.

The original plan was to take the boat over to my dad's barn but that was not going to work. But my friend agreed to let us keep the boat there for just one night and he wanted to also gp. The next day the farmer who I had paid to carry the boat to the south end showed up at the place we agreed to meet. However the farmer was not on the wagon and sent another man we didn't even know. This of course was suspicious to us because if it was some one we didn't know that could be dangerous in time of war.

We did not have much choice and as it turned out we couldn't have had a better person than Arie who was a thin but serious lad that didn't have much to say and we were not into talking much, we needed help so we proceeded to pick up the boat at my friends barn. We immediately found out the cart was to short for the boat so we had to find some planks to extend the cart. Fortunately we found heavy planks near the barn and we proceeded to slide the boat onto the cart. We covered every thing with straw and the cart was ready to leave as soon as the curfew was lifted for the day.

We didn't travel with the cart because that would have raised too much suspicion. He had to pass through five check points but he traveled that route many times and the Germans sort of knew him and would just pass him through. It was a wet and stormy day which was a advantage for Arie because this would leave the check point guards inside their shelter and just wave him through. We all traveled different routes to our place where we would unload the boat. We had spades and tools on our bicycles to show that we were heading to a work site for the Germans We really didn't have our proper papers to where we were heading so we had to bluff our way through the check points. At one of the check points we had to put on a act that the bike was broken down and we had to fix it right by the gate, The guard finally got tired of us working on our bike and told us to walk through the gate and never even asked for our passes.

We had agreed to meet at a place where where there were no mines but the cart stood out on top of the dyke road so we had to move fast to unload the boat from the cart. We had to temporary hide the boat until the curfew time came that eve so we covered it with the straw from the cart so it looked like a pile of straw sitting out in the field. We hid in a ditch until it got dark so we could start moving the boat out towards the water. It was a long way and we had to cross a mud flat to get to where the water was deep enough to float. We loaded our bicycles on the cart for Arie to take them back to the farm because we couldn't just leave them there and arouse suspicion. It was then when Arie told us he was coming back and join us in our escape. We promised we would wait until he returned. We really needed his help in moving the boat to the waters edge.

We could hear the tanks across the water and and were so close and yet so far. The Germans were patrolling the road and we had to time our movement in between patrols to move the boat. Across some ditches and then finally to the mud flats. We were now closer to the water where the Germans were patrolling the water in power boats. It was a real job pushing and pulling that heavy boat and stopping and listening for any patrol. Then we ran into another major problem the mud was so deep we could hardly move the boat as we sank into the mud. We would sink several feet into the mud which made it extremely difficult to move the boat. But as we got into the water the boat became easier to move because it started to float but not enough for us to get into it.

Kees had brought a bottle of Dutch gin this really gave us a needed lift. It was dark and we were cold and wet and covered in mud. Kees insisted on bringing his bike so that was in the middle of the boat along with some of the straw. The boat was now in deep enough water to where we could climb into the boat and start paddling We had made some paddles because the oars that came with the boat would be way to noisy. So we started to paddle and keep it a s quite as possible. Bram the guy who worked on the ferry boat put up his hand and said to stop, we were not paddling equal and were starting to go in a circle. So we had to work out a system where we would do five paddle strokes and stop to work out a rhythm system.

As we slowly approached the center of the channel we became more confident, this was when Bram raised his hand and said to stop and listen. We couldn't hear anything but Bram who was more attuned to the noise of river traffic said he is hearing the chug chug of a German patrol boat and it was heading straight for us. There was no way that we could paddle away from the area so the only thing left was to pull in our paddles and lay low in the boat and just pray. It was a moonless very dark night and about all we could do was just let the boat boat float like a lose row boat if it was spotted. We agreed if we were spotted by the Germans we would go over board and swim for shore. This was great for the two of us but the other two guys couldn't swim. Something we never thought about. We didn't dare make any movement and just waited as the patrol boat got closer and closer and their boat was almost on top of us. But then the sound then started to fade as the patrol boat passed us by, they had not seen us. We slowly sat up and couldn't believe it, we felt like shouting but we looked at the shore line and started to paddle as fast as we could. Then all of a sudden the boat hit the shore line. It was good timing because it started to get dawn light and we could see outlines of shapes on the road along the shore line.

There was a drain outlet that ran into the water and we pulled the boat into that , As we looked up we could see barbed wire all along the top. Kees was the only one of us that could speak some English and shouted "is any one there?". They opened up with some machine gun fire, it was a wonder that no one got killed. That response was totally unexpected and I immediatly threw myself over the side into the water tipping the boat over. We were all in a now complete state of shock. Kees the shouted "God save the King" and that might of saved us. We were ordered forward as we scrambled up the bank as the Canadian soldiers covered us with their guns. We didn't know what to expect now, we were wet and covered in mud and cold.

We were taken to a farm house that was close by where the Canadians had taken over the farm where the farmer and his family were present still in the house and were taken to the kitchen for a mug of hot sweet tea. The Farm yard was full of tanks and military vehicles and the Canadians told us they had never seen anything like what they were looking at, most of the people that have come across were German soldiers. The Canadians were kind enough but very firm and we were treated like prisoners, we felt let down and it was not until later when were questioned that we understood why we were treated like we were. Germans were coming over pretending to be refugees but really intended to spy for the Germans.

We were taken by jeep to a camp to be interrogated. There was a real mix of people they were interrogating including women with their heads shaved for being German sympathizers. They interviewed us one at the time but they kept Bram for a long time because of his work on the ferry boats bringing German soldiers to the island. Bram was able to give the Canadians some very useful information. While we were there we heard and saw the continuous flights of the VI flying bombs that came over our area on their way to London. We were there just over night and then transferred to Rosendaal where we were questioned again by the intelligence service who wanted more detail on what was happening on our island.

This was when we finally got to know a little about our latest member Arie who it turned out had a similar background as myself. His family moved to the mainland when the Germans flooded their farm but Arie stayed and went to work for another local farmer Geert Jacobs who was allowed to keep his horse and wagon to supply the Germans with food. He then became involved with the Dutch resistance passing on vital information about the Germans. Since he was driving the cart he was allowed into places where the local people were not allowed. It was a perfect situation for him to gather information for the Dutch resistance. He realized his days were probably going to be numbered and anyone caught doing what he was doing it was instant death.

I found him to be a truly great character we had both seen the breakdown of life as we knew it . Family, community and religion had all been important to us since our childhood but the German occupation had brought different values that we found hard to accept. We wanted our families to know that we were safe and Kees arranged for a message to be sent out on the radio. He had to word it very carefully so nobody would be incriminated. He simply said. "Everyone at Risico is Happy". Risico was the name of the boat.

While we were at Rosendaal we heard that we had some copy cats who tried to copy what we did, but the Germans were more alert and they were caught and executed. The bodies of ten men were left hanging near the market for three days. We then didn't feel so proud of what we did after we found that out. We also found out the eight friends who were going to go with us and then chickened out were all rounded up and sent to a German labour camp for the rest of the war.

The four of us split up, Bram went to Antwerp to join the merchant marines and became the captain of a oil tanker, Kees went back to the farm where he had looked after the farmers onion crop and seed and was looking forward to doing that. Arie and I joined the Dutch Army again and for a while were in charge of clearing the german mine fields while the Canadians continued to battle the Germans and slowly continue their occupation of German held positions in Holland.

Arie and I didn't stay long with the Canadians we were transferred to Wokingham England where we met up with other Dutch troops. We did managed to see London and look at the devastation the VI flying bomb did to the city. Huge sections of the city were destroyed and there was nothing but piles of rubble. We were to report to Liverpool and embarked on a ship to Malaysia. They issued us tropical kits and clothing for the hot climate. Our destination was Sumatra one of the Dutch colonies. The war in the East with the Japanese was over and the Dutch were ready to resume their oil and tin and many sought after Items for the Dutch economy.

We were told the Japanese had surrendered and we should have no trouble but we knew there were still active Japanese troops on the island and to them the war was still ongoing. We had to fight snipers and guerrillas who were fanatics and our job was to stabilize the country and protect the citizens I stayed there until my injured back got so bad to remain in the army and I was also fighting malaria and was sent home on a hospital ship. I was thirty years old and then spent two years in a hospital back in Holland since the war had ended there.

Nellie and I were married in 1950, and our daughter was born two years later. There was still tension between my brothers on the farm and I needed to make a change. Well the huge flood of 1953 devastated the Islands and everything was under water, so there would be no farming for a couple of years. It was then that a drainage company asked me to drive their drainage machine for them. Well the government took away the subsidy and I brought the machine to England to pick up some business over there.

I started there in 1959 looking for business in the Lincolnshire area. It's near the city of Boston a huge area with a similar terrain as Holland and in great need for drainage. Business was good so I brought my wife and my now two daughters over to England. From that venture of running a drainage machine I started my own company building drainage machine with the help of a good friend and partner who was a engineer. The business just kept growing and we ended up as a supplier of drainage machines that ended up all over the world. I still return to Holland to visit but my home is now here in England.

Bram Dykers, Kees van de Doel, and Arie Holleman. I'm extremely grateful to these three men. I would never have managed to escape without them. And I'm sure they saved my life because two days after we left the island in that old row boat there was a huge round up of all eligible men that were sent to work in the labor camps in Germany.

After the war Han would often come by ferry to visit his friend, Cor, in Oudenhoorn. Han also made sure to get together with my cousin Neeltje and it was during those visits I came to know him better. Han and Neeltje married June 15, 1950, about two years after we moved to America. Their daughter Lindy was born March 21, 1951, and Agnes a few years later. Lindy became manager of her dad's business until he retired. Han passed away in 2018 at the age of 97.

Mastenbroek drainage equipment

Chapter X – GIRLS, BOATS AND GROWING UP

At about the age of twelve we boys were being taught sex education in school but it was only the basics. Our REAL education came from girls who were now hanging out with us on almost a daily basis. All of us boys had part time jobs working for farmers or merchants and always had some spending money of our own. Two of my friends, Cees R and Will B, and I, along with three girls, Corrie O, Bep B and Cobie K would ride our bicycles to Hellevoetsluis where the only movie theater was in our area. Because Hellevoetsluis was about ten miles from where we lived we would only go there during summer months.

The movies we saw were either British or American, subtitled in Dutch. We boys, of course, wanted to see American cowboy movies but the girls were more into serious and romantic films. At the theater we would pair up with the girls and it didn't take long before it became sort of a steady boyfriend - girlfriend thing.

It seemed that the girls were a few years ahead of us boys when it came to sexual knowledge. They had magazines, books and Hollywood photos acquired from their older sisters and probably fantasizing things we boys never even thought about. They were far more sexually inquisitive than we boys and often talked among themselves, sharing such information. This was not something boys did. We were into fishing, building things like boats and exploring the countryside.

At right and next page: Magazines of the nature girls brought to the loft.

One of our group of boys worked for a dairy farmer who had a barn with huge hayloft. He was allowed to go into the barn and play in the hay without having to ask the farmer's permission every time. One day he invited all of us over to the barn to show us what he built in the hayloft. He had dug out a area almost like a private room and we couldn't believe it was completely hidden from view. I'm sure the farmer didn't even know it was there.

The girls evidently thought this secret room was the perfect place to put their plan into action and wanted to play 'hospital'. Of course they were the nurses and wanted to examine our bodies, putting their hands everywhere to check us all out. This was truly sex education and the girls were having a ball. We boys played along with their doctors and nurses game to see where it was going to lead. The girls were far more interested in see us boys naked than we were them. This may have been because their bodies were not yet fully developed.

At right: Pin-up photo typical of those in magazines brought by the girls.

Our times in the hayloft usually ended up with a lot of kissing and feeling. I would now call it making out. Good thing was that we were still too young to create any pregnancy problems. These were definitely the wonder years – wondering what was going to happen next. All this fun went on for almost a year but ended when my family and I traveled to America in 1948.

It was probably a good thing we left when we did because I could have gotten into some real trouble with the girls. I never found out how it all ended or if someone else came to replace me. Years later I heard that Cees R and Cobie married and had some kids. On one of my trips back to Holland I met up with Cees and Cobie. We had a short visit at the ferry terminal as I was leaving Holland for England to visit relatives. I communicated with Cees for a while. He always had a desire to come to America but couldn't afford the trip. Cees wanted me to pay for his travel, thinking I was a rich American who could easily do just that. I never took him up on it as we really were not that close. Also, Cees had some medical issues and wasn't even working. I later learned that Cees passed away at a relatively early age.

Boating must naturally be in our blood for being raised in Holland meant you always lived on or near water --- usually a small canal. As such, my friends and I had a never ending thirst to build a boat. Most of the time our efforts were confined to only constructing rafts because we did not have access to material needed to seal planks on our home built boats. Tar was about the only thing available and we did not have means to heat it well enough to pour. Consequently, most of our boat building ventures ended in failure.

Boy in home made boat

A typical raft effort

One day one of our gang said he saw an old bath tub sitting in a farmer's cow pasture and thought it might make a fine boat. When we went to check it out we couldn't figure why a tub would even be there. It certainly couldn't have been for watering cows. Where we lived there was no need for fencing to contain livestock as fields were separated by drainage ditches or small canals. All a cow had to do was go to the waters edge to drink. In our minds the tub was just something someone had thrown out and wouldn't be missed if it was 'borrowed' for a boat.

A small canal was not far from where the tub was located and the water was only about four feet below ground level. It would be no big deal to get the tub to the canal and slide it down the bank for a launch. Or so we thought. We soon learned the tub was made of cast iron with cast iron feet. That meant it would be quite heavy and, with the attached feet, very difficult to slide over the ground. A big problem.

After a lot of planning we figured to accomplish our new venture we just needed the proper materials. We promptly set out to scrounge up some poles, big planks and ropes to move the tub from where it sat to the waters edge. Getting the tub to the canal would be one thing. Sliding it down the embankment was quite another. It needed a lot of control to keep the heavy tub from going too fast into the water, possibly capsizing and sinking. With a lot of rope secured to the tub, and more than a bit of hard labor on our part, we got the job done.

Once we had the tub floating we immediately discovered it was not stable and could tip over very easily. And, if it sank the tub would be almost impossible for us to raise from the bottom of he canal. Using wooden poles we constructed outriggers on each side of the tub to stabilize it so it wouldn't tip over and after a few adjustments (adding more poles for flotation) our boat was ready for 'sea trials'. Final touches would be making paddles and putting in wooden boxes for seats. We were ecstatic! We actually had something that would float and not leak.

My rendering of our bathtub boat

Over the next few days we tried out our new boat, with friends all given rides. Proud of a job well done we were ready to show our handy work to the village that was about a mile away from our launch site and off we sailed. Word was out that those crazy Vanderwaal kids had built a boat from an old bathtub and a bunch of townspeople were waiting for us to show up. Our boat was quite the novelty and it seemed everyone thought we had had a great idea. Well, not quite every body. News had spread about our bathtub boat and it didn't take long before its owner learned where his tub had gone missing. All too soon we had a very irate visitor at our house.

The farmer who owned the tub had come to tell my dad that we had stolen his tub. After a lively discussion between him and dad the farmer said he would not press charges against us if we put the tub back exactly where we had found it. We told dad we had just borrowed the tub for some fun but that excuse didn't cut it. Following some very heated input from my dad, though totally devastated, we 'agreed' to the farmer's terms.

Little did we know we then had a project even more challenging than launching the tub. The heavy cast iron tub would have to be pulled back UP the bank of the canal. That would require a lot more hands and we set out to recruit our friends for help. After all they too had enjoyed boat rides. Putting planks, poles and ropes back in place we proceeded to put the tub back where we got it. Getting that tub out of the water and up the bank was a lot of pulling and pushing on everyone's part and it took us a couple of days to complete the task. We were not sure which hurt more, our bodies or our pride but there is one thing of which I have no doubt. That farmer must have enjoyed every moment watching us put his tub back. Today I would love to have pictures of our great sailing adventure.

And this is how I remember getting that heavy tub out of the canal.

We boys didn't always engage in mischief as we grew up. Though religion was not a big factor in our family we did attend our local church every Sunday morning and went to Sunday school to learn basics of the Bible. It was sort of routine, like going to regular school. There was only one church in the village and it was of the Protestant faith, as were most people of our village. Catholics traveled to the next village where there was a Catholic church. Most small villages were structured this way. I know that as a baby I was baptized in that church because I still have a certificate of the event. I'm not sure if my two brothers were baptized or not.

Besides school, church and trying to stay our of trouble, there were a number of other fun activities we often enjoyed and should be noted. Then, of course, there was work.

A very unusual hobby for many kids was collecting paper and/or thin metal bands that circled cigars, a hobby that dates back to the late 1800s. Popularity increased as printing became more colorful and detailed embossed bands with lots of red and gold were introduced. Bands are so collectible because they look like miniature pieces of art. Also, they illustrate the cigars place of origin as well as its brand. Though many cigars were made in Holland, most came from Cuba and other countries. Kids would try to collect as many as possible of the wide variety of bands from all over the world. Cigar bands were usually displayed in a special book and traded very much like kids in America trade sports figure cards. Many kids my age got a good start by having a collection passed down to them from their dad or a grandparent.

Many of the older generation of men enjoyed a good cigar and they were readily available from local tobacco shops. Some tobacco stores would sell bands without the cigar. Birthday parties, weddings, holidays, or any event were people gathered were popular with the adult crowd and they were frequent. These were when guys would have an excuse to congregate for a drink and good cigar. They were also great times for us kids to collect bands from the cigars adults smoked.

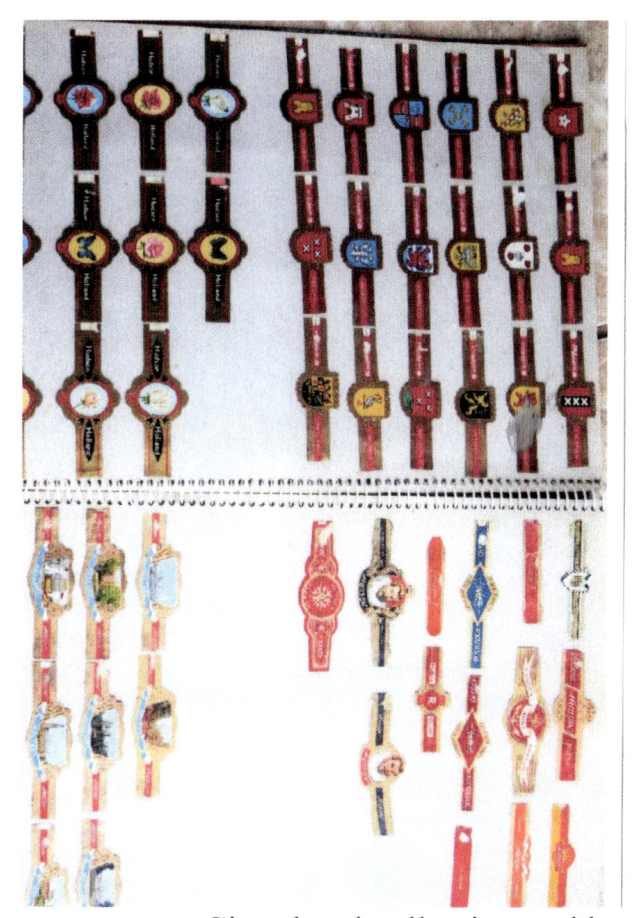

Cigar band collection and how they come wrapped around cigars

Holland is known for the ever presence of strong winds that would cause fallen snow to drift across ditches-and canals, creating tunnels for us to walk through. During those cold days we usually wore our wooden shoes with straw added inside for insulation and to make them more comfortable. Winter was about the only time we boys could wear long pants as they generally are not worn until manhood.

Wooden shoes for everyday use.

Cold winters meant we could do a lot of ice skating and travel long distances in the frozen waterways or canals. Ice hockey was played when we got a bunch of kids together. I still have my old Dutch wooden skates with steel runners that were held to the shoe with leather straps. These were the forerunners of modern shoe skates.

Skates like I had when I was a kid.

Another way we traveled over the ice was on a small sled called a 'stekker'. It was a very low sled with steel runners like ice skates. You would sit on the stekker, feet forward, and propel yourself with two short spiked poles. Or, you kneel on it which would gain you more speed. If you were really good you could obtain speeds on a stekker almost as fast as a skater. We had a couple of stekkers at our house when I was growing up. I'm not sure if my dad made them or if they had been passed on to him from someone in the family.Dutch stekkers.

Dutch stekker

Though stekkers have been around for about 200 years they don't seem to be used much in Holland these days. They have really gained popularity in Korea, however, especially among the younger crowd.

Korean stekker sledding

When canals were frozen deep and safe enough for heavy loads an annual event called the 'Elfstedentocht' would take place. Elfstedentocht means 'Eleven City Tour' and the biggest and longest speed skating competition in the world . The tour is over 200KM with skaters traveling over canals and lakes through eleven cities from southern to northern Holland and back. Wimps need not enter.

Elfstedentocht Tour

A small picturesque lakeside city on the northern part of the tour is Hindeloopen. In February a huge winter festival is held in Hindeloopen and coincides with the Elfstedentocht. Part of the festivities is that the townspeople dress in 'turn of the century' costumes and have a grand skating party. They also use and display very old wooden stekkers, many of which are hand carved and/or finely decorated. Some even have a backrest built on them.

Hindeloopen festivities

Antique stekkers with backrest

Little brother Hugo was about two years old in the Spring of 1948 and could walk. He then wanted to be with the big kids all the time and follow us everywhere. This became a bit of a problem because, though he could walk okay, he wasn't that speedy.

My friends and I decided Hugo needed a ride so he could keep up with us at least some of the time. We then designed and built sort of a pull cart/ wagon for him.

Since there wasn't much available in the line of materials to make what we really wanted we improvised with some boards and an old wooden window shutter. And, using the wheels from an old baby buggy mom had, we put a cart together.

Hugo and his pull cart

Hugo was a happy kid when we pulled him around in his cart and loved to go fast. The faster we would pull that thing the better he liked it. Fast must have stuck with Hugo since that early age because later in life when in America he started 'drag racing' cars and entered local events.

When Hugo's two sons came of legal driving age he built two drag racing cars called 'rails' and raced them at drag race strips all over the country. Hugo even made custom vehicles to haul the dragsters. A motor home like cabin was built on a flat bed truck and after that a special trailer was made. It was a fifth-wheel type trailer with sleeping accommodations up front for the boys and the back large enough for the two race cars. They would be gone for weeks when going to different racing events and instead of staying in motels they would stay in their own rig. Hugo ended up building a half dozen of that motor home cabin on heavy duty flat bed trucks for other guys who pulled their big trailers that held race cars.

Hugo's race cars and trailer

During the two years prior to our traveling to America I worked in the field for various farmers. A large crop on the island, in addition to potatoes and onions, was sugar beets, The beets had to be thinned in the spring after they came up from seed and again when they grew to be about four inch sprouts. If not thinned the sugar beet would not grow into a big beet, Sugar beets were often huge, with many well over a foot long and heavy. Thinning was a 'hands on' operation where you straddle the beet row and, by hand, pull out the extra sprouts so the single sprout would stand alone to grow into a huge beet. In the fall when the sugar beets matured and plowed out of the ground I would help with the harvesting. In later years this all became mechanized with huge tractors doing all the work. I usually ended up on the wagon in which guys would toss the beets for me to rearrange for a maximum load. This too became mechanized, as did loading and topping.

Since harvesting took place in the fall it seemed that it always rained and made loading a real muddy mess. When we got home mom would tell us to take our, messy, muddy, dirt caked clothing off outside before she would wash them. Beets were a very important crop for making sugar. They would get taken to a processing plant then cooked into a syrup that was converted to sugar.

Sugar beet thinning

My dad made deliveries of sacked potatoes to the city driving an old military surplus Studebaker truck the Van Hennicks acquired right after the war. Dad would often load the truck during the day then drive it home in the evening so he could get an early start in the morning.

There were days while on my off times from school or work I would get to ride with dad on his deliveries. I loved riding with dad because we got a chance to talk, one on one, and would usually stop somewhere for lunch or a treat. Before dad took the truck back to the Van Hennicks' warehouse he would drop me off at the house. Wonderful memories.

Dad in Van Hennick's Studebaker

Chapter XI – OUR DEPARTURE AND ARRIVING IN AMERICA

Following a bitter winter of 1944-1945 and the end of war in 1945 many people were seeking any and all means to provide for themselves and their families. There was economic upheaval and mass unemployment throughout Holland. It was the toughest of times. By spring of 1948, several families in our village had left for America, including the Bevaart family who had a couple of daughters about the same age as Cor and me.

The Holland America Line, a Dutch shipping company, and a number of other shipping companies made ships available for those who wished to migrate. Their ocean liners would transport as many as 2000 passengers per ship to destinations such as Australia, Canada and the United States. Over 500,000 immigrants left Holland to seek employment and a new life in those countries. It was a migration of people that lasted about ten years.

In late 1947 dad informed his employer, the Van Hennicks, of his plans to migrate to America. Dad had worked for them since 1924, after completing his sixth grade school requirement when he was 13 years old. The longer dad worked for the Van Hennicks he became more aware that he was in a dead end job and staying there would mean he could never achieve anything more than being a common laborer. Compounding the problem was that the Van Hennicks' son was the same age as dad and destined to take over the business. There had been rivalry between dad and the son, with constant squabbling going on between the two. It was just going to be a matter of time before dad wouldn't have a job if he had to work for the son. To make matters worse dad was bringing work problems home to my mother and we kids even knew what was going on.

All this came about the same time dad's sister Dirkje, who was living in America, came to visit all her brothers and sisters. The timing was very fortunate for dad as he and Dirkje had some serious conversation about his job and she convinced him to move to America where would have the opportunity to achieve his goals in life.

On the downside, however, with all the service men returning from the war there was a massive unemployment situation in America. The United States government had put in effect placed immigration quotas that limited how many people could come into the country. That caused many immigrants to go to Canada or Australia where there were no quota systems. Nonetheless, Dirkje finally convinced dad to apply for immigrant status because there was a loophole in United States quota system he could use. The country had a shortage of dairy farm workers/milkers. Dad convinced the government officials he could fill that position because he was raised on his dad's small farm where they had dairy cows he milked since a young child. Dirkje also sponsored our family, at the time a requirement necessary for coming into the United States, and dad's immigrant status was accepted.

My aunt Rena, dad's other sister who owned a small restaurant in the city. Rena had previously traveled to the States to visit her brother and sister for a couple of months. She also had friends in New York. Rena laid all the groundwork for our arrival in America and helped us out financially. Dad then made travel arrangements for the trip and secured necessary documents. We then had to have physicals and a series of shots required for travel to America. Our reservations confirmed we were slated to leave in July of 1948. We had about six months to dispose of our furniture and goods, pack for the trip and say 'goodbyes' to all. This was a huge move for us kids. It would be the adventure of a lifetime and we were looking forward to the trip.

Our house when we left for America

Reservations for our trip to the United States were made on Holland America's ship the MS Veendam II, an older ship that survived the war. During the war it was used as to accommodate German officers and off duty sailors. It had been extensively damaged but was rebuilt as a cruise ship.

The Veendam II was originally built at the Harland and Wollff Ltd. shipyards in Glasgow, Scotland, in 1922. She was 576 ft long and had a beam of 67 ft. Her four steam turbines engines would produce a max speed of 15knts. It had a capacity of 1898 passengers and crew of 328 --- 263 first class, 435 second class and 1200 third class.

SS Veendam (1922)

SS Veendam as we saw it

The ship resumed service in 1947 to ferry immigrants between Europe and the United States. Her final voyage was in 1953 to Baltimore where she was scrapped. (We later sailed on Holland America's newer Veendam IV on its maiden voyage from New York into the Great Lakes in 1997).

Months prior to our trip mom, dad and us kids made the rounds of visiting all of our close relatives and friends. This was also a chance for mom to show off the 'Sunday' suits she had made for us boys. Although nicely done, there was a bit of misjudgment with those suits. They were the style popular in Holland and France at the time but, as we found out later, never adopted in the United States. More on that later.

It was time to sort out and decide what we were going to take to America. Dad had wooden crates made to pack belongings that were special to the family. And, only being allowed a couple of large trunks or crates, what we could pack had to be precise. It also had to be done carefully so fragile things like pictures and keepsakes would get there in one piece. Mom's sewing machine, of which she was so proud, had to come with her and got packed as well.

Sewing machine like mom's

Mom was an excellent seamstress as she had been sewing since a young girl. She loved to sew and make clothes from pattern books. Learning to sew was very common for girls in Dutch schools. When mom completed school at thirteen years old she immediately went to work part time for a local farmer. She was then able to earn and save money until she had enough to purchase her own sewing machine. It was a very well built portable Singer machine, operated by a hand crank and came with a beautiful wood case. Mom would sew clothing for herself, her sister, and mother and in a household of seven boys there was always a lot of mending. Making patterns and applying them to the fabric used for sewing was her favorite pastime. A strange coincidence is that after I graduated High School I was hired by the Boeing Company and my first job there was a pattern maker. Patterns I made were of metal, called templates, and used to make most airplane parts. I guess cutting patterns must have run in the family.

A few days prior to leaving we were really busy saying our goodbyes to neighbors and close friends, particularly the close friends we had been running around with the past two years. Most people wished us good luck and a great trip. Some were a little jealous of us leaving on a whole new adventure. We promised to try to stay in contact once we were settled in America but, somehow, not much of that really happened. It was probably due to us being in a completely different world and time taken to make the transition.

Ten years later mom and dad returned to Holland for a visit. Brother Hugo, who was 13 years old at the time, went with them. By then I was married and Cor in military service. During those ten years dad, who started out as a dairy farm milker, had been extremely frugal and saved enough to buy his own dairy farm with a herd of cows. Because they were sure a lot of friends and relatives had real doubt about them leaving Holland they couldn't wait to get back to tell of the success they enjoyed in America. Dad particularly wanted his old employer, the Van Hennicks, to know how well he had done for himself.

Our departure for America was from the Holland America pier in Rotterdam. On the day we left a large crowd of relatives and friends gathered to see us off. A good share of mom's family, including her mom, dad, sister Marie and Wim were there. On dad's side of the family were sisters, brothers and cousins. Look closely at the group picture made on the day of our departure and you will see the special suits mom made for Cor and me.

Family and friends seeing us off.

Our favorite cousin Corrie was there with her dad and mom, my dad's sister Trien, Aunt Trien was a year younger than dad but married a couple of months before he and mom were married. Corrie was only a few months younger than me and, because our families visited often, we grew up together. She was very close and who we would miss most. *Of note is that Corrie started accordion lessons about the same time we left for America and later in life played the instrument professionally. Corrie performed throughout Europe either stand-alone or in a combo on special occasions. She was on radio programs, made TV appearances and produced numerous recordings. Corrie married her manager, Fred Bourgonje, on December 24, 1957. Interesting is that I married in November of 1956, just a year before Corrie did.*

Corrie and accordion

After our goodbyes to family and friends who came out to see us off we boarded the ship on a large gangway and were welcomed aboard by one of the ship's officers. One of crew then took us to our cabin. The ship sailed that afternoon and by morning we were tied to the dock at South Hampton, England, where additional passengers were boarded. That evening we departed for our twelve-day crossing to New York.

Hard to see, but here we are, on the gangway being met by ship's officer.

There was good weather for one day after departing England and a smooth ride while along the Irish coast. The next day we participated in lifeboat drills. Everyone was required to put on life jackets and gather at our assigned lifeboat. A day later, as we were well under way, the weather took a turn for the worse and we started to get some really rough seas. Waves were breaking over the bow of the ship and no one was allowed on deck for the next few days. Mom and little brother Hugo, who was only two years old, got really seasick and stayed down in our cabin the whole while. Being third class meant we were berthed in the lowest part of the ship, which wasn't all that bad as far as riding out the rough seas. We actually got a better ride than the first and second-class passengers who were in upper deck cabins.

On the deck. Mom holding Hugo.

After riding out the rough water we got a break in the weather and allowed on deck again. Mom and Hugo also felt much better as they could get out of our cabin and get some sun. Mom was able to meet and talk with other lady passengers about where they were from and where they were going. Cor and I changed to our Dutch short pants and felt a lot more comfortable wearing them. Even with that mom and Hugo still spent a lot of time in their cabin so Cor and I were always bringing them bread rolls and sandwiches. Dad spent a fair amount of time in the men's lounge where he could sit, have a cigar and, over a glass of beer, swap stories with other guys.

Cor and I met some other kids about our age and went about exploring the ship with them. We went into places we were definitely not allowed as third class passengers (us) were supposed to stay out of the first and second-class facilities we sneaked into. Food in the third class dining room was not the same or as good as in first and second-class dining rooms. Acting as though I was a rich kid I would sneak into the first class dining room by standing in the food line with a family that had kids and join right in with them. This was fairly easy since there were a lot of families with kids on the ship and I was never questioned. Once inside I would look for the desert table, help myself to goodies that weren't available in our dining room, and when the coast was clear make off with a hand full. I would then take some down to Mom and Hugo who were wholly surprised and wondered where we got those delightful treats.

We boys had a lot of time on our hands and besides exploring the ship there were some other things we could do. Being as a lot of families were aboard there was a social director for kids and they tried to keep us occupied. Movies were available in the afternoons and on deck there were games like shuffleboard. We somewhat enjoyed the movies but the games were mostly for younger kids and we weren't interested in participating. There were about as many girls on the ship as there were boys but other than just talking to them there was little else we could do. Not being of the same age group as the girls, unlike the movie *TITANIC*, I had no romantic encounters. There were also English language classes we could attend and that was very useful. We didn't know a word of English because it was not yet a school subject we were exposed to in Holland. Today English is a mandatory subject for every child in Holland. Most of the time we tried to stay out of trouble and away from the ship's crew who were always trying to keep us from places we weren't supposed to be.

Couple of handsome dudes posing on the ship.

Some days we had sunny weather but others were rain and wind. It seemed like the trip was taking forever but eventually we could make out a coastline and then the buildings of New York City. It was still early in the morning as we entered the harbor. Almost everyone was on deck to see the Statue of Liberty as we passed by but it barely visible due to a light fog. We knew we were almost there when tugboats showed up to assist us to our mooring berth.

Statue of Liberty

Our family didn't have to stop at Ellis Island where other immigrants had to get a medical examination and any shots they didn't have. We had all that done in Holland prior to our departure. Plus, my dad's sister sponsored us. Prior to the war there were very little restrictions put upon immigrants but when we arrived a sponsor was required before being allowed into the United States.

Ship passing Ellis Island

It wasn't long before we received word to gather our belongings and prepare to disembark the ship. WE WERE IN AMERICA!

Later in life I saw the movie *TITANIC* and it brought back a lot of memories of our trip to America, especially of the ship being class divided. I'm happy to note our trip had a much better ending. The Veendam, the ship on which we sailed, was somewhat similar to the Titanic in that both had black hulls. However, the Veendam was shorter and only had two smoke stacks whereas the Titanic had four. The Titanic also had coal-fired engines much larger than those in the Veendam, which were oil fueled. The Titanic was constructed in 1909, thirteen years before the Veendam being built in 1922.

After disembarking the ship, gathering our luggage and clearing customs, we met up with dad's sister Rena. She was going to take the ship back to Holland the following day. We were sure glad to see her and her New York friends because we couldn't speak a word of English. They took us to the train station by taxi and made sure we were all set to make our three-day trip to the west coast. Since they knew language was going to be a problem they had prepared a huge sack lunch that was to last us the entire trip. However, peanut butter and bologna sandwiches were things we had never eaten before and not fond of, but ate them anyway. Of course we boys were all over the train meeting people and it wasn't long before we found a family who could speak both Dutch and English and helped us order meals in the dining car.

When we started out on the train and got a real look at the countryside we realized this was not the American cowboy movies portrayed --- or even close to looking like the old west. And mom became concerned that they had made a huge mistake because parts of the cities the train traveled through were not exactly picture pretty. In fact, they were the worst parts of America. What a disappointment! However, things improved as we came further west and three days later we arrived at our final destination; Auburn, Washington.

Upon our arrival in Auburn we gathered our luggage, had the two wooden shipping crates unloaded and off-loaded the train. The date was August 6, 1948 --- fifteen days from the day we left Holland.

Dad's brother Cees, his sister Dirkje, and some of their children met at the station. Cees and Dirkje were older than dad and had migrated to America in the 1930s. Aunt Dirkje had married a Dutchman who was in the livestock hauling business. They had three grown children. Uncle Cees was a dairy farmer and had one son. Both families were living in the community of Enumclaw. Upon our arrival we stayed temporarily with aunt Dirkje because she had a huge house and her children no longer lived at home.

Aunt Dirkje and uncle Cees had arranged a new job for dad, as well as for a house we could rent in the town of Auburn, which was about an hour's drive from Enumclaw. Dad went to work as a dairy farm milker for a Dutchman named Pete Schoordyke. This was a complete career change for my dad and a whole new way of life.

First house in States

A final note on clothing issues Cor and I were having during our travels. As previously told, before we left for America mom made us new suits in the latest style in Holland at the time. The suits had trousers with 'bloomer' leg bottoms that stopped just below the knee and looked a lot like what golfers wore. They were totally unlike anything we saw boys wearing. It wasn't long before we noticed people staring at us and kids questioning where we were from to be dressed in those pants. Being continually embarrassed, that did it! We told our folks we no longer lived in Holland, we were now in America, and didn't want to be teased about wearing strange looking pants.

That ended our worldly travels and we happily retired to our beds knowing days ahead would be filled with wondrous new adventures*.

*Adventures documented in my first book – **THE FLYING DUTCHMAN.**

Our family in front of our aunt's house right after arriving in Enumclaw.

Dad with his brother Kees and sister Dirkje

When my brother and I awoke that first morning after our arrival at my aunt's house we looked out of the upstairs bedroom window. What we saw in the distance was the snow covered Mount Rainier. It was like a fairy tale come true! To this day that mountain has always been a reflection upon our good fortune and a beacon leading us into the future.

Mount Rainier

We never realized it at the time but coming to America was probably the best decision our parents had ever made. Being in the States my brother Cor later changed his name to Corky and I had my Dutch name, Jaak, changed to Jack.

EPILOGUE

Looking back at the early part of my life while living through the German occupation of Holland I can now reflect how fortunate we children were those years. Specifically, of note is the following:

First, living is a small village away from the horrors of war throughout Europe allowed a safer childhood.

Second, being as young as we were we did not have to bear the fear experienced by older kids who could be readily drawn into the war.

Third, we were very fortunate in that we did a lot of things older kids probably would not have done or gotten away with.

The experiences we had and chances we took as children during that period followed me throughout the rest of my life. I had become inured to risk and well reflected in my first book, THE FLYING DUTCHMAN, about my life after moving to America.

ACKNOWLEDGEMENTS

My thanks to Bill Grostick for editing and assembling the data and pictures for this updated edition of JAAK, a story about my life during the WW II German occupation of Holland.

I also wish to extend my gratitude to Lin Robbins, former secretary at my place of business. Lin's insight and assistance was equally invaluable.

Additional sources of information and/or reference:

Cami Brecto of Camirenee Fine Art for the cover illustration

"Of Dutch Ways" by Helen Colijn

"Lets Go Dutch" by Johanna Bates

"Oudenhoorn een Agrarisch Dorp" by J Zeelenberg

"We Marched against England, Operation Sea Lion 1940-1941" by Robert Forczyk"

"Once Upon A Wartime" by Molly Burkett

"Nieuwenhoorn- Flotbrug in vroeger tijden" by Eammerzael Mooldyk

"Wikipedia" For additional information